FIRMER FIGURES

FESS UP OR MESS UP

How to spot the signs that your small business is failing so you can fix it before anyone finds out

By Georgette Rowland Osborne

COPYRIGHT

DEDICATION

To my lovely husband Gary who has lived through my obsession with business people and their money. And to my grown up babies Myles and Jess; who have become accustomed to the back of my head and the light from my pc. I love you.

To the entrepreneurs out there that go through so much in pursuit of a dream life and the desire to do the best for their families; and in the world. I admire you.

ABOUT THE AUTHOR

Georgette is Director of the Financial Gym, and Precision Services Outsourced Bookkeeping. She is creator of the Firmer Figures Framework for entrepreneurs. An author and speaker.

In addition to her professional qualifications, Precision Services is a regulated practice. Georgette was also invited to join the panel of experts for Guardian Newspapers Small Business Network.

Georgette began her working life in catering management and then decided to enter the cutthroat world of IT and Finance in Central London at a time when it was not the easiest place for females to belong, let alone one from an ethnic minority. However she thrived there and became manager of a bespoke IT outsourcing company in the City with banks her main specialty.

She was head hunted by a rival company because they wanted to get into the Bank of England and Inland Revenue (as they were called then) and both had made it clear they dealt with her or not at all. She resisted until the company she worked for was forced to close due to money mismanagement. She took a colleague from the previous company with her and together they introduced a new suite of products and services that changed the structure and direction of their new employers. Georgette was also responsible for the relationships with many other major corporations including Merrill Lynch, NM Rothschild, NatWest Bank amongst others; and ironically, HMRC or the Inland Revenue as they were called then.

Before finally leaving the corporate world Georgette was part of a management team tasked with growing a company that had been a loss leader for its previous owners. The company trained engineers around Europe to install setup and maintain critical server based computers such as ATM machines and Air Traffic Control. This venture was an alliance with Compaq Computers who had bought the other part of the company for the hardware technology.

Of her achievements in the corporate world, the one that she is most proud of is proving that even as a woman, with a young child, and only working part time, you can still compete. She became the first person in the organisation to produce revenues of 6 figures per month on her own as well as with her team and as she puts it "still be home in time to cook dinner"

She later went into business with a friend in an industry she knew nothing about. It turned into a nightmare which almost ruined her financially. She went from physically fit to extremely overweight.

After getting tired of licking her wounds she decided it was time to not only sort out her weight, but to also launch her own business, so Precision Services was born. She also accepted two company directorships; and took on overflow work for an accountancy practice in prestigious Harley Street to build up cash until she had the reserves to go it alone.

When she read a statistic that one in three businesses do not make it past

3 years old, she knew that for so many this could be avoided with the right information at their fingertips. She had personally been through it. She also realised that so much of what made her successful in big business had no place in small businesses, there was a different, tougher set of rules and few safety nets. She discovered so many business owners who came from the employment world and despite being in business for some time were still making the same mistakes with very little support.

The similarities between the lessons, experiences and strategies she had to use to get out of financial trouble and get back her fitness levels are the inspiration behind the Financial Gym which is more a labour of love. It exists as her platform to help business people become smarter at spotting and avoiding financial danger signs in their business before it is too late.

Georgette wants to take the fear out of finances and believes that until people put as much energy into understanding the money, as they do into designing a logo or website; she has her work cut out.

FIRMER FIGURES

TABLE OF CONTENTS

INTRODUCTION

So you want to start a business? You have had the concept for a sure-fire successful business for a long time and you have cultivated the idea into a viable business plan and, the possibility of working for yourself is something that you relish. You are dying to take the plunge but something is holding you back.

Realistically, it can be good to be cautious and to really think through all of your options prior to taking the plunge. Working for yourself has many benefits of course but you can't just concentrate on the positive aspects of being self-employed, you need to look at the demands of such a business as a whole.

When you work for yourself, it's true you can – eventually, set your own hours, you get to see the fruits of your labours but you typically have to work very long hours especially in the early days when the business is starting out. You will be juggling jobs, feeling the pressure of keeping everything moving in the right direction and as the days roll into weeks and months, those long hours can take their toll. No more clocking off at 5pm, you finish when the work is completed.

Starting up a business in this financial climate is hard work, even more so if you are working solo or managing just a small team of people. It means that all of the responsibility and pressure sits on your shoulders. You have to be a business analyst, a marketer, a director, a manager and you have to budget and manage those financial accounts too.

If you have worked for a large company you will know that everyone has their set roles within the organisation. When you go into work you have a job description that details your work remit. Your managers delegate to you and you complete the tasks accordingly. You know that your area is just one small cog in a large organisation. If you perform your tasks to perfection, this well-oiled and productive cog fits in seamlessly. When you work for yourself, you have to cover a wide area of expertise which is not always easy in terms of time management, work-flow and ability because it can result in you stretching yourself to the limit and juggling the business operation ineffectively.

So many people rush into setting up their businesses that they do not always forge the strong foundations that are needed to then be able to build a financially sound enterprise that can grow from strength to strength.

This book provides sound advice suitable for business start-ups irrespective of the type of business. This is because it provides the nuts and bolts required for any new enterprise and includes crucial advice on planning ahead and what is needed to achieve success in a fast and ever - changing financial climate. It stresses the need for an innovative business plan which forms the framework for future success. It discusses the importance of identifying and understanding your market and researching out your potential customers or clients.

This book explores the character types of business owners and entrepreneurs, so that you can identify your own weaknesses and strengths and understand the best way for you to operate. It provides valuable information on when and why you should outsource as well as the importance of learning to be adaptable and flexible to change. Change management skills are essential for the new business owner and if you can embrace this aspect of your skill-set from the start, then you will be able to flow with the changing economic tide.

If you could have a personal how – to manual on managing a business efficiently and effectively that detailed the business growth, how to build the essential layers of a sound business quickly and easily, you would probably jump at the chance. If yes, then this book will fulfil those requirements and will become a detailed resource that scrutinizes the business world, helping you to evolve your business ideas so that they grow into well-researched products or services. This book cuts through the commercial quagmire surrounding business start-ups and instead cuts right to the chase, identifying the areas of concern that must be considered for the business if you wish it to be successful. This book also looks at the pros and cons of business partnership and how to ensure that any potential disharmony can be avoided.

Firmer Figures provides personal tips and highly relevant case studies that endorse the message throughout and provides a valuable guide for new business owners and existing ones who wish to improve their efficiency and financial rewards whilst streamlining the process of business management.

CHAPTER 1

Know You Are Up To The Challenge.

Start at the end – by deciding where you want to end up.

If you are still in employment and are earning a regular salary, you have the luxury of being able to plan your business before you get your feet wet. If however you are already in business, you have the advantage of real life experience to fall back on. Going back to basics gives you a chance to reassess whether you are on track with your original plans or even if your original plans still make sense.

Having met with business owners in the course of my work I have been privy to the most sensitive information about their financial headaches. Over and over again, I listen to the frustrations that business people face because they feel they are not in control of their financial future, despite all their hard work. There is often a strong sense of embarrassment or even of feeling like a failure

I try to ascertain their business needs right from the start and together we discuss their long-term projections, not in terms of the type of legal structure, e.g. self-employed or limited company etc; but in terms of the physical manifestation and their personal reasons for this. We assume that earning a living is a given, but it is rarely the main reason that people decide to work for themselves.

Knowing that other motivations go a long way into understanding what a particular client would see as a solution to their problem, I can often help by looking at the nuts and bolts of their company requirements with an experienced and analytical viewpoint. Dreaming about what our businesses will be like is inspiring at the start of the journey. We have wonderful plans of the money we will make, the lifestyle we will have; how proud people will be of us. How proud we will be of ourselves and so on. An entrepreneur, who wants to support a particular cause, is focused on different things to one who is more inspired by building a business empire. For those who are looking for more freedom over their future will have different needs again.

The responses are varied but there are those that crop up time and time again and these tend to fall into 3 main categories. The first question to be asked is:

What type of business is seen as the one to aim for?

Inheritance – Passing Down to Family

One of my favourite business experts Robert Craven had me in stitches at one of his events a few years ago when he said that on retirement or death, most business people would be lucky if their business was worth more than a paperclip – or words to that effect.

While at the time it seemed a controversial statement, the statistics do bear this out. Why is this? Are we just no good at building businesses that can feed our families into the next generation?

Not at all! The problem does not seem to lie in ability, but in the approach. We say we want to build a business to pass down as a legacy, but proceed to create something that only works well if we are in charge of it. The business is built around the knowledge, skills or qualifications of the owners, so without them the business would cease to exist.

Even those that have employees, often have a culture built around one individual. If you cannot go off and leave your business for at least a week so that it continues to earn an income, and you are safe in the knowledge that day to tasks still get done, then it is not a business. Let alone something to pass down. It is a vehicle to earn income for you but that's it.

Lifestyle Business

Traditionally the term 'lifestyle business' has been used in almost derogatory terms to describe those people who seemingly play at their business just to support their particular way of life, they are seen as people who are playing at business in order to support a particular lifestyle.

Traits are as follows:

- There is little chance of being of value

- It is often one of the hardest business structures to achieve successfully

- There is passion over pay

- Often referred to in condescending terms as less of a business than others, but many do make good money particularly if in a specialist industry or niche.

- Primarily established to fund a life choice

- An actual hobby, a pursuit or a skill that may require more funds than were anticipated originally by the owner so they have to work harder to earn the money. Exactly what the owner tried to avoid.

- Where the pressures of covering living expenses may add unanticipated financial stress, particularly if not accurately accounted for prior to starting out.

- There is a reliance on family resources, e.g. one person is the main breadwinner while the other runs the lifestyle business. If the breadwinner loses their job then what? The lack of urgency to earn money gives a false sense of security.

Some reasons for this choice include:

- The decision to pursue a particular hobby and make money from it

- The chance to use skills that has been stifled by employer(s).

- Where an income is required 'at home' so they can be around whilst their children are growing up.

- A chance to escape the "rat race"

- In pursuit of the elusive "work/life balance"

The credit crunch however has seen many "back-up breadwinners" lose their jobs and so the pressure on the family unit is intensified, forcing the lifestyle business owner to make changes they did not anticipate. Some even are forced into considering going back into employment.

- For others, the actual hobby or skill they wanted to explore turns out to eat money a lot quicker than they can make it, so what once brought pleasure now brings pressure.

- The sheer responsibility of covering living expenses may end up overshadowing any desire to pursue a lifestyle dream.

This is describing a lifestyle business in terms of popular perception. However the majority of businesses are actually lifestyle businesses, though many entrepreneurs would deny that their enterprise falls into this category.

Startlingly the majority of entrepreneurs that start out with the intention of creating a legacy business are unable to make the leap so create what is in essentially a lifestyle business that has no future unless they are still part of it.

Please do not run away with the notion that lifestyle businesses are inherently flawed. They are the backbone of industry and many are very successful, and enable owners to make a very good living for themselves and for their employees.

They can span from sole proprietor and home business, e.g. plumber, graphic designer, IT engineer, life coach, retailer, estate agency, car mechanic/body shop to a larger organisation. What they have in common is less about what they do for a living and more to do with how they do it.

The lifestyle business is based around one person doing practically everything. Or it could be a business with staff but most things have to go through the person in charge; basically the owner is almost indispensible. There are critical jobs that go undone if they are absent, and often the actual product or service cannot be produced or carried out without them, and this means that no income can be made.

Few tasks are systemised or automated because there is "somebody" on the payroll who does that and they know most of the work "in their head". The payment of bills dominates the business rather than the shoring up of assets, even in businesses that make profit. However this is often due to how the money received is managed and the owners' attitude to money in general. More about that in later chapters.

The percentage of credit and borrowing is not offset by assets, e.g. assets being the things the business owns, money owed to business from customers and including the cash in the bank. If their credit facilities were ever to be withdrawn, it could mean the difference between staying in business and closing down.

Investment is usually not an option because there is insufficient potential profit or capability for the business to grow for an investor to realise a decent return, so such a business would not interest them.

They imagine that when they have had enough they will be able to sell their business. But when they try they are shocked to find that they have few takers. If there is interest, the buyers offer much less than they hoped. Also they may be required to stay in a business even after the sale because it is so dependent on them that a substantial hand-over-period would be needed.

A Business That Has Potential to Grow, Make the Owner Rich And Create a Dream Lifestyle

A Business of Tangible Value

When financial experts assess the current and future potential success of any business, there are three main areas that they look at:

- Profitability

- Potential for Growth

- Cash flow

How much profit does it make? Is it just covering overheads or is there enough surplus profit to pay the owners a substantial bonus and to still have enough money to fund investment, acquisition of equipment and other assets?

If someone were to invest in them is there enough profit to enable the investor to get their original investment back plus interest?

The more profit, the more likely it is that a business can attract investment or be eligible to borrow. However if they are making a substantial profit, the need to borrow is greatly reduced.

I firmly believe that borrowing should be to fund something that takes you to the next stage; not for the purposes of just covering day-to- day expenses. Too many businesses are reliant on their overdraft and credit facilities.

In times of adversity such companies are vulnerable because banks start to cut back on lending and even withdraw credit facilities altogether if they see evidence of weakness in the company's finances, as we have seen during the recent credit crunch and recessions.

For many businesses, this means the difference between survival and collapse.

Financially robust companies have reserves in place to draw on during tough times, because the level of profit has enabled them to divert money into assets and investments as a matter of routine.

The second area is potential for growth, or scalability. Can the product or service be sold on a much larger scale? How easy would it be to expand the company's products or services? Can the whole business be replicated as in franchising or can what it offers be taught to others easily?

Entrepreneur John Warrillow defines a business of value as one with products that are:

- Teachable

- Repeatable

- Valuable (in the minds of customers)

- Scalable

Growth could be a substantial increase in volumes of sales, a greater market share, or the expansion of the actual organisation; so that it sells by the sheer fact there are more resources to handle additional business. If that growth is managed well, the natural outcome is greater profitability leading to more cash available.

This takes us to business success indicator number three – cash flow. This is the amount of money available to a business at any given time. Astute businesses know what cash is needed to meet its financial obligations at a point in time and can predict whether they will have enough available to cover those obligations.

The people who plan for this type of business structure are serious about planning for the future. They are setting things up in such a way that there is a good chance there will be something left for their heirs. If they decide to sell, there is a greater likelihood of not only finding buyers but realising a good price for the business that results in a cash payout rather than being obligated to stay in the business to assist in a hand-over.

According to Experian and other leading business statisticians, only about 5% of businesses ever achieve this type of structure.

Good Business Idea – You May Not Be the Person to Run It

Research! Research! Research!

If you have a new idea, you need to check whether there really is a market for it. If there are other players in the industry, what are they doing, and how successful are they at it? What will you bring to the party that is different or better than what they are offering?

Plan! Plan! Plan!

Because I do not want to deviate from the core purpose of this book, I will not spend too much time on this topic, as it is a subject area in its own right. But the importance of creating a business plan cannot be stressed enough.

It can be the length of an A4 sheet of paper right through to a multiple page document. The form it takes largely depends on the purpose and the reader it is intended for.

You may have a business plan to be used internally just by you to ensure that you stay on target with the direction of your business. A plan designed to secure investment or borrowings will be presented in a format that contains information that is attractive to investors, banks and other lending institutions.

My day to day business plan is in the form of a chart, because even though I love figures, I am naturally a visual person, so seeing something at a glance appeals to me. Another form of this would be a mind map. However I have also produced quite comprehensive business plans because it helped me to thrash out the details behind an idea.

There are a number of online sources that will give you a good template for a business plan, some are free.

If you are honest, realistic and you do the research necessary to produce a workable business plan, then you should have been questioning yourself all the way through, and in turn coming up with viable solutions to any areas that did not seem do-able.

The business that I am in now has changed quite a lot from the one I started. Even though the purpose behind the business has not changed, the way it is carried out, certainly has, and my plans and forecasts are updated to reflect this.

Has your home business changed from one that was planned to make a simple living, and has turned into a business that now employs staff? Have you realised that your business works better with outside rather than internal resources? Do you perform better as a broker rather than the actual service provider or vice versa?

Seek Out the Opinions of People in a Position to Give You Constructive Criticism

- Family and friends are not necessarily the best people for this

- Criticism will encourage you to substantiate your idea or business on a practical level. Others may see things that you do not because they can be more objective.

- It will test how well you can deal with rejection, how de-motivated you can become and how quickly you bounce back.

- Rejecting your own ideas. Instead of focusing on the dream (goes against all self-esteem advice) focus on what could go wrong. The weaknesses in the idea, deficiencies in your skill-set, insufficient finances, inadequate support systems, lack of available resources. Then work out how you are going to combat them.

I use the word "criticism" deliberately. It is one thing to challenge our ideas on a personal level where no-one else knows what we are doing or is unaware that we may have very real doubts and concerns about whether we can pull something off. When the only voice we hear is our own, it is easy to convince ourselves that we are on to a winner.

To be exposed to the scrutiny of others is to open a whole can of worms that sometimes proves too much for any prospective business owner to overcome.

When we start our businesses we see them as our babies, and that is often exactly what they are – an extension or an incarnation of ourselves. But this is the very thing that frequently prevents a business from achieving success.

It is startling just how many business owners live in perpetual fear of failure, and are worn down by day-to-day stresses, constant struggles, and they experience difficulties in making ends meet, and feel lonely and isolated, not knowing where to turn for help. But they end up doing nothing out of embarrassment or deeming they cannot afford to find a solution.

The explosion of information, particularly on the Internet, in some way has made things worse for many. Believing there is less excuse for not having the answers and for being able to get everything done, solving every issue themselves as material is so readily available.

There was the tragic story some years ago of the millionaire who killed his family; and himself rather than face the ordeal of dealing with his massive debts. Now I struggle to understand why he chose to take the life of his family, but the despair that he must have felt is familiar to many business owners and whether you are dealing in hundreds of pounds, thousands or millions of pounds, the journey from pressure to misery to giving up hope can be shorter than we think.

Story Alert

I get involved with people starting businesses all of the time. By pure coincidence, while I was in the middle of writing this very section of the book, I received a message from a contact of mine who had been the accountant employed by one of my clients until they had left to work at a company nearer to their home.

I shall call him Jordan. Jordan is a qualified accountant and years before I had trained him on how to use Sage accounts and payroll when he was still working for my client. In turn, he had hired my payroll service at their new employer when a key member of their accounting team left. Help was needed until they were able replace them.

Jordan was disillusioned working for other people; and wanted to explore self employment and asked if we could chat about it. He planned to take on clients slowly in his spare time while still working until such time he could afford to hand in his notice.

We met for a coffee and the first thing I asked was how he saw his business even in the short term? Would he be working from home from the back bedroom or renting office space? Did he go out to clients regularly? Did he plan to work on his own or would he be looking to possibly have another person working with him at some point?

Jordan had no idea.

I decided to leave that one for now and asked if they had given any thought about what they planned to offer. Accountancy covers a multitude of services and I stressed the danger of just being another one on the market.

In fairness, this is a challenge for many people starting out because we can be so fixated on what we know and fail to translate that into what it means to a client. We are so busy telling people "I do this" rather than if you deal with me "you get this."

As we talked three things became apparent:

1. Jordan was not so much interested in starting or running a busi-

ness of his own, he was more interested in getting out of employment. Working for himself seemed to be the logical next step..

2. No real thought had gone into what it takes to be in business for yourself and what preparation would be needed. Even though Jordan is a great accountant, he had always worked as an employee doing accounts for one organisation at a time. He had never had to deal with the issues of many clients simultaneously and had little appreciation of how different that is.

3. When I started out, I had built up a number of contacts over a period of time that were already doing business with me, and others who I knew would come on board. Jordan had none of these and I realised he was hoping that I could give him a magic way of finding clients that would be small enough to be serviced easily in their spare time. In fact that was really the only aspect he had given any thought to at all.

To be blunt Jordan had no clue where to start because he was still being propelled by emotion only. However even though it was not the prime motivation, when Jordan asked for my input, he was covering one of the fundamental bases. Seek out people that will ask the awkward questions and force you to address them.

Family and Friends

Family and friends make good sounding boards, however also be aware of the opposing forces of those closest to us. There are good and bad points.

The first is the "I will support whatever you do". On the face of it, this would seem to be a wholly positive stance. But the problem rests in the fact that such a stance is not objective. Unwavering support does not ask difficult questions.

However, in times when things are not going according to plan and you need encouragement desperately, these people prove invaluable. Importantly, you can rely on them to promote you to others.

The other comes from those that are customarily critical of you or if not of you, of new things or simply of change. While it is prudent to understand that there may be negative reasons behind their responses, do not discount what they have to say. Sometimes just the act of proving them wrong is incentive enough to get you off your behind and to deal with any weaknesses in your plans.

Expert Opinion

These can be other business people, industry experts, potential investors, and potential customers.

They are not encumbered by any personal feelings towards you; so can concentrate on the business viability of what you are proposing to do. This process can be nerve-wracking, particularly if you are seeking the opinion of those you have a great deal of respect for and it can be quite devastating to have them pan your idea.

Business coaching, mentoring and counselling aimed at getting a person emotionally and psychologically ready for business is an industry in itself.

Yourself

It is one thing to listen to other people, but ultimately the decision for how you move forward comes back to you because it is you that is going to have to make things happen. Often when we come up with a plan for a business or start trading, our expectations are at best unrealistic and at worst completely off track.

The original plans may have been more to do with ego, desperate circumstances or taking advantage of what seemed like a great opportunity, amongst others.

If you have taken the time to pick the business idea apart, whether before you start or after you have been in the business for a while, this will allow you to build stronger foundations with which to move forward and it will make it more likely that you will accomplish what you set out to do.

Emotional and Mental preparation

Prepare To Make Sacrifices - Strong Commitment

Despite the experiences we hear about from those that have gone before about how hard it can be to be your own boss, few are prepared for the reality of just how hard it can really be.

- Long days, constantly working – at least in the early stages

- Missing family time and feeling guilty

- Feelings of being overwhelmed

- Copious amounts of energy needed, but when it does wane, be committed enough to ride the storm

- Mastering the art of being an effective manager of time rather than overwhelmed by the lack of it

One of the great ironies of deciding to work for yourself is the idea of being more in control of your working life; but time and time again when I meet with prospective clients one of the recurring themes is their feeling of being out of control.

Much like childbirth, no matter how much people try to describe to you what it is like, you never really understand until you have gone through it yourself.

Even though you are prepared to work around the clock 7 days a week, it can be tough to leave home before your children have woken up and arrive home after they have gone to bed. Even if you work from home, being holed up in the spare bedroom hearing the rest of the family get on without you is testing for many.

My test was my daughter who would always burst into my home office at precisely the time I was in deep concentration and I would lose my train of thought. The amount of times I would get irritated with her and then feel guilty because all she wanted was a hug. I would then indulge her for a whole lot longer than I had planned, just to make up for it and then completely lose where I was, give up and go and make a cup of coffee.

There you have one of the biggest factors – guilt. We console ourselves by proclaiming that it is for our families, when it is all too often our own dream we are fulfilling, which adds to the guilt. Even though ultimately we do want to improve the lives of those around us, when the guilt sets in, it is easy to question whether we are doing the right thing.

It is even harder if your family were used to certain aspects of your life that have been put on hold while you ramp up your business; e.g. family holidays.

There is no right answer, just the one that works for you. But if the entrepreneurial path is the one that you really want, then do it with all you have because if you are going to make big sacrifices, be sure you are really committed. That is one of the traits that my clients all possess.

Story Alert

I took on a client a little while ago that had been referred to me by their lawyer. The company was extremely busy and everyone was rushed off their feet so the admin and bookkeeping was always behind and they had constant cash flow problems. We sorted out the backlog and arranged a meeting to discuss where things were, and how they wanted to proceed.

One of the directors arrived early and while waiting for the other one, we just started chatting about how things were going in general. As the conversation continued I could hear his voice changing and I realised he was on the verge of tears. I looked at him and asked how often he felt as he did now and had to push the feelings back down, and right on cue he broke down.

"You waited a long time to do that didn't you?" I said and he nodded.

"Well the thing you dreaded doing most has happened, you have broken down in front of someone you didn't want to and I haven't run out screaming so you might as well let it all out"

Bless him, he was mortified but smiled and said "If you only knew".

But I did know, not only because I deal with people in his position on a regular basis, but because I remembered what it was like to be in his position.

What he was dealing with, was a mixture of feeling overwhelmed and of inadequacy. He was working around the clock, very few decisions were taken without his input, he barely saw his family and though they paid the staff, the directors had not paid themselves anything in months. Added to the fact he had borrowed from family members to buy his share of the business, he was scared stiff of losing their money and being perceived as a failure. The pressure was making things strained between him and the other director.

He said that he was worn out and if he had known what he was letting himself in for he would not have become involved.

He had become so bogged down with his situation that he was no longer able to see the positives. They had an established business with good and regular clients. Granted there were some major changes that needed to be made but what a good place to start.

Accepting Advice and Guidance is not a weakness

His lawyer recognized that he needed to reduce his workload and recommended my services. To their credit they were only too willing to explore other ways of doing things. It is amazing how many business people are stuck doing things their way, because that is how they have always gotten by.

. No matter what problem or situation you are facing in your business whether it is a small matter or a major obstacle. Rest assured someone has dealt with it before and successfully. The worse thing to do is struggle on alone trying to figure out an answer to a problem that someone else has already figured out. The skill is in finding them.

Just because you are the only person in your business, the director, the person with whom the buck stops, you still need people to support you and people to look to for assistance. Surround yourself with people who can do the things you are not so good at.

Able to Take Rejection and Deal with Setbacks

It is tempting to avoid the opinions of others because you want to avoid feeling rejected. You are being judged after all and few people welcome that. And worse, possibly by someone whose opinion means a lot to you. Keep your perspective and be honest with yourself. It may not ease your own disappointment at their reaction. Remember however, the more you do to change your life, the more likely you are to deal with the doubts of others...

Resourceful

There is more than one way to skin a cat as they say. If plan A, does not work, you should always have a plan B. The need to be resourceful comes as a result of unexpected success as well as hard times. You suddenly get a big order that you didn't expect to win and you do not have enough staff or supplies to fulfil it. How you solve this may make demands on your creativity, support systems, and finances that take you well outside of your comfort zone.

Adaptable To Change and Not Dogmatic About The Way Things Need To Be Done.

How often do we bemoan what it is like working for and with people who can only ever see their own way of doing things, while conveniently ignoring the fact they we can be that way ourselves? This is particularly if we have been working in an industry for many years and we are dealing with others who do not have the same level of experience. It can be very tempting to dismiss ideas and suggestions that do not seem feasible to us. But if we were to have an open mind it is amazing what new ideas we can benefit from that we would never have come up with on our own.

I remember a morning brainstorming session with management consultant Andrew Priestley, who is someone I have the greatest respect for. Having a pair of fresh eyes coupled with years of experience brainstorming with me took me down avenues that I had totally forgotten or overlooked.

What Level Of Income Do You Need To Live On? Drop In Earnings V. Employment

It is frightening how many people go head long into starting up their business without knowing what money they will need to survive and how they are going to cover this amount while the business builds up. If you have managed to put funds aside to cover your living expenses while ramping up then you are ahead of the game.

What Level Of Income Do You Desire?

It is one thing to know what money you need to live on at the moment, but that's the boring bit. Concentrating on what level of income you truly desire is not only much more inspiring, it is fun. It should also serve to push you to create the type of entity that will achieve this for you

Financial Planning

Understand what financial information you need to get up and running and to grow. You do not need to be an accountant, but if you do not have a handle on the money continuously, you will lose the grip on your business entirely.

This we will tackle later in the book.

CHAPTER 2

Business Behaviour Effects on Performance

As discussed earlier, the vision of a business that the owner had at the beginning more often than not bears little resemblance to the business they end up with.

One of the fundamental reasons for this can be found in how the business is structured in the first place. Now while the results are not the same in every case, there is very strong evidence that the type of structure you create can greatly influence how likely you are to achieve your goals. Even down to how you end up spending your time.

Let me illustrate.

Solopreneur/Self-Employed Behaviour
Structure of Self-Employed / Solopreneur / Sole Trader

- Most common type of business structure to be based from home

- One person takes care of all aspects of the business or may have a member of the family in a support role. E.g. mobile car mechanic whose wife takes messages and sorts out the paperwork – pardon the sexist stereotypes

- Financed by owner's profits, savings, overdrafts and bank loans

- Basis of the business is usually a skill or experience in an industry that they were successful at while employed

Characteristics of Person/Circumstances

- Do things much the same way as others in the industry and difficult to distinguish business from other similar ones

- Focuses on finding more work rather than finding profitable customers

- Associate working hard as the key to success

- Networking and word of mouth is the main way of getting business

- Being in control is a key MOTIVATOR

Pros And Cons – Why Choose This Structure?

Pro – You keep all the profits

Pro – Compared to other business structures the paperwork and record keeping is more straightforward

Pro – The affairs of sole traders are kept private.

Con – All debts are yours and you can be held personally liable for the repayment of those debts even if that includes risking your home

Con – More difficult to obtain credit or funding so growth can be restricted

Con – The entire burden rests on the shoulders of one person

Usual Outcomes

- End up doing the essential work themselves

- Reluctant to let others do essential tasks as doubt they will do it as well as them

- The business is based around them and is only as strong as they are

- Believe outsourcing is not necessary when they can "do it themselves" despite the fact that tasks are left undone when they get busy

- Have very little influence on their industry so react to industry trends rather than to set them.

- Despite possibly being in a worse financial position compared to when they had a job; they assure themselves that this is preferable to being employed.

- Likely to fail within a few years of starting up because it is not only dependent on one person to do everything but requires them to have all the expertise needed to sustain the business long term.

- Become seminar junkies always looking for the next big idea that will transform their business but rarely make any fundamental changes.

Business Grafter Behaviour
Structure of Grafter Business

- Typically a limited company or partnership, but can include sole traders e.g. retailers

- Made up of 2 or more people

- Generally work from premises rather than from home

- Business is run by directors on behalf of the owners

- Financed by overdrafts, bank loans and profits.

Characteristics of Person/Circumstances

- Set out to actually create a business rather than just a vehicle to make money

- Rely heavily on their experience of being employed and consciously or subconsciously recreate much of that

- Believe they can do it better, "I have made money for other people now it is my turn," is not an uncommon statement

- Believe in finding the right staff for the job

- Set out to do things better than their employers but have no clear plan of action as to how to make that happen.

- More interested in what they have to offer and how good they are at it

- Convinced they will get business because of how good they are at what they do

- Have a decent website and a social media presence and they do some marketing. Effort is stepped up when business is slow and drops off as they get busier.

- Constantly looking for that key to success that will take the business to "the next level". Is it the right person, the right technology, the next great product or service?

- Seminar junkies like their self-employed cousins and come away with renewed vigour and motivation to get stuff done. But once back in the office, the pressures of day to day work push the plan of action down the to- do-list and that is likely where they stay.

- Make lots of changes with no real idea as to how those changes form part of an overall strategy for improvement, so they slowly but surely end up back where they were.

- Fail to attract the type of people they need to work with because not willing to spend the money. Sees paying for outside expertise as taking the food out of their mouths.

Pros and Cons – Why Choose This Structure?

Pro – Because directors determine level of salaries and dividends paid – it is possible to pay lower taxes than a sole trader with the same profit

Pro – The name of a limited company is protected

Pro – People other than the main shareholders can own shares in the business e.g. employees, investors, family members

Pro – Considered a more steady entity as the business is a separate organisation to the owners, shareholders and directors, (frequently all the same people) and so exists in its own right

Pro – All debts belong to the company so the personal wealth and assets of the directors and owners are protected

Pro – Some expenses that are considered private expenses of a sole trader are considered legitimate, tax deductible expenses of a limited company e.g. drawings versus salaries

Pro – Viewed as more stable than a sole trader business, so easier to borrow

Con – Business affairs are in the public domain

Con – Directors are bound by legal duties and can face penalties if they do not adhere to them.

Con – The bookkeeping and accounting procedures of a limited company are subject to more complicated and restrictive rules than those of a sole trader.

Con – Have to deal with corporation tax as well as personal tax and the added costs associated with their preparation

Usual Outcomes

- Many of these businesses carry on and provide the owners with a good living and may only end because the owners decide to close the doors or if they pass away.

- Because they are set up around the skills and knowledge of the owners and directors and run this way on a day-to-day basis, they are rarely able to be sold.

- If it is a family business then the option to hand it over is an option, but the business can only continue for as long as there is someone willing to take on the relentless hard work. How disappointing to have a business that you dream of handing down to your children; only to find out they have no interest in it because they see it as a trap rather than an opportunity.

- Regardless of how long the business has been established, the relentless hard work shows no sign of reducing, and each passing year becomes another one that looked much like the one before.

- Not uncommon to decide that they made a mistake in the beginning and decide to change the business entirely or shift to a different industry in the vain hope of getting it right this time. But invariably repeating what they did before but without the support of all the groundwork that was already in place with the previous business or industry.

- Because the foundations of such businesses are commonly weak, e.g. reliant on overdraft/credit to finance the daily activities, dependent on the owner/director doing so much of the work or decision making that it cannot function without them. Any adverse economic and market conditions could push it over the edge.

- Who outside of the financial circles could have connected the dots in the early days of the recession between U.S. homeowners in the sub-prime market and your business bank reducing your overdraft or refusing you the loan that you thought was a done deal as it had usually been in the past.

Business Savvy Behaviour
Structure of Savvy Business

- Typically a limited company or partnership, but can include sole traders e.g. retailers

- Made up of 2 or more people

- Generally work from premises rather than from home

- Business is run by directors on behalf of the owners

- Financed by overdrafts, bank loans and profits

- As time passes positive results may attract outside interest on a small scale; such as individual investors or business angels and joint ventures

Characteristics of Person/Circumstances

- This type of business owner/director has much the same behavioural characteristics as the business grafter however

- They have a more structured approach to the different elements of their business. They see the benefits of removing themselves from the non-earning repetitive tasks that the self-employed and grafter business owners cling to with such determination.

- Advocates of seminars and workshops like the self-employed and grafter business owners, but are more likely to actually implement some of what they have learned

- They recognise that they do not know it all and that there are people out there who know more about certain aspects of business than they do; even, in their own area of expertise

- They see the spending of money to improve the business as an investment rather than a cost, but often fail to direct this money to the right things due to lack of experience and knowledge

- Willing to not only seek the expertise of coaches and mentors but takes subsequent action

- Actively delegates and uses outsourced service providers as a way of attracting the skills and resources they need without the hassle of doing it themselves; and can understand how the long-term benefits can outweigh the actual costs.

- Business is run using efficient systems and automated processes designed to maintain a consistent approach to roles and tasks, not dependent on who carries them out

Pros and Cons – Why Choose This Structure?

This is exactly the same for the aforementioned Grafter Business.

Usual Outcomes

- Attain a much greater level of success than the self-employed and the grafter businesses, but more than likely they still do not accomplish the hopes and dreams they had originally envisaged when they started out.

- To other businesses and competitors they may appear to be doing very well, but if you were to scratch beneath the surface you could find much to indicate otherwise. The decision to sell or an attempt to secure investment are a couple of the scenarios that can expose weaknesses in the business that were not previously obvious. Except maybe to the owners themselves, though I know from personal experience the owners are time and again the last to know.

I recently worked through a budget and cash-flow forecast with a director and his general manager who had been going for more years than they cared to mention. They were shocked to find that even though money came in regularly they were making losses on a regular basis too and it was only because they collected holding deposits up front from clients that they always seemed to have lots of cash.

The only reason they addressed it was because when the recession hit, a few of their clients closed their accounts due to their own financial issues. In a short space of time the business had to refund quite a substantial amount of these holding deposits which had in turn caused financial problems that had not been an issue since their early days. Worse still, they had no immediate way to resolve the issue because they had not anticipated the possibility of being in this position.

On deeper investigation other related problems were uncovered which resulted in the company having to take drastic action to reverse the rot.

True Entrepreneurial Behaviour
Structure of an Entrepreneurial Business

- Less than 5% of businesses are really entrepreneurial

- Typically a limited company or partnership. They rarely stay as sole traders.

- Made up of 2 or more people

- Generally work from premises other than home.

- Entrepreneur conducts a great deal of business on the move.

- Business led by entrepreneur(s), run by managers and/or team of people with strong relevant skills and experience.

- Financed by overdrafts, bank loans, profits, shares and outside investment, the type of business most likely to interest venture capitalists

Characteristics of Person/Circumstances

- Motivated by greater purpose than just making money (though not in all cases). Have a vision

- Not necessarily more intelligent than other business owners but consciously decide to think and approach situations differently

- Accept that they do not know everything they need to know, so actively seek out others who can fill in the gaps

- Desire to satisfy the needs of a group of people, running a business is merely the method they choose to meet these needs

- Strong ability to put themselves in others shoes and so structure offerings to appeal to their target audience

- Constantly looking at ways to improve and innovate with the need of the customer being the prime driver

- Some have talent for spotting opportunities and positioning themselves ready to take advantage of them

- See taking risks as part of the game, although the risks are calculated to propel the business forward

- View failures as temporary setbacks – learning curves as part of a journey; not outcomes in themselves.

Usual Outcomes

- Become leaders in their field

- Others try to copy what they do but rarely achieve the same level of success because they do not share the same outlook on how businesses are run

- Visualising outcomes way beyond what others believe is possible allows them to create entities that are profitable and positioned for massive growth. Even though they may be vulnerable in the early days with regards to available cash, they are able to turn this around in abundance as the vision moves closer to a reality and additional "believers" want to be part of it.

- Who they are; what they do and what they stand for is very clear to interested parties e.g. customers know what to expect in their dealings with them, investors take an interest because they can make educated assessments as to the potential returns on investments.

- Opportunities come to them as other businesses see the benefits of being associated with them – opening up other ways to make money.

- Running such businesses are extremely hard work and require immense energy and focus, but the rewards – financial and otherwise make it worth it.

- Entrepreneurs are most likely to truly find their business fun to work on.

CHAPTER 3

Step Back To Gain Control

The likelihood of financial success is not the only area affected by the choices we make in how we set up and run our business. The actual day to day experience and enjoyment differs widely between the different types of business structures.

As stated before, these examples do not apply in every case. They are just the most likely experiences of the people in each particular group.

A Week in the Life of the Sole Trader / Solopreneur / Self-employed

- Work from computer/laptop in home office or spend day out on "jobs" depending on line of work until well into the evening

- Self-improvement or business building event/workshop

- Paper work and admin gets in the way of improving the business or generating sales, often carried out during unsociable hours and frequently not up-to-date

- Irregular time off for holidays as business cannot function without them or, no money is made in their absence.

- Time off is not enjoyed because unable to switch off from the business mentally as always so much to be done

- Marketing and Social Media activities

- Patchy social and family life, due to lack of free time – fitted in when often too tired to fully engage in any activity or company or to be able to communicate with interest.

- Attend networking events and business breakfasts

- Catch up on accounts/bookkeeping

- Juggle finances and chase customers for money

A Week in the Life of Grafter and Savvy Business Owner

- Open office or business premises each day – usually first to arrive and last to leave even if employs staff

- Delegate tasks to staff and supervise how they are carried out

- Deal with customer issues

- Deal with supplier issues

- Juggle finances – negotiations with bank to ensure have enough operating funds.

- Able to take time off but regret it on returning to work. Face a mountain of problems generated because they were not at work to personally "keep an eye on things"

- Waiting for record keeping, accounts to be brought up to date so can make some financial decisions.

- Attempt to deal with the forms, red tape and compliance requirements required by the HMRC and other professional bodies relevant to their industry.

- Fire fighting caused by unforeseen circumstance, e.g. client complaints, staff absence, equipment breakdowns

- Meetings

- Marketing and Social Media activity

A Week in the Life of a Successful Entrepreneur

- No such thing as an average or typical day

- Meetings and negotiations regarding future opportunities

- Meetings with collaborative team(s) to discuss project progress and further ways to improve on delivery and customer experience.

- Review of latest financial reports and data to see if revenue, profit, sales and cash flow are on target

- Analysis of financial data with financial support team, e.g. book-keeper and accountant, maybe management consultant also.

- Travel on business to enhance profile and generate further income

- Long days compensated by fantastic breaks away to recharge batteries ready for next period of hard work.

- Enjoyable social life, exposed to a large number of like-minded people in the habit of experiencing the nicer things in life.

- Can afford more time spent for personal hobbies: gym membership, golf, musical aspirations.

- Do not go to office every day

- Possible media requests and interviews based on reputation as an expert in field

- It is easy to see that the true entrepreneurial set up is the one that is likely to be the most rewarding, not just from a financial perspective, but for the personal well-being of the owner/director. But why is this?

- There are a number of factors that influence this but for the purpose of this book; I will concentrate on the one that is dear to my heart.

The Art of Letting Go

If done properly, the benefits of letting go can transform an overwhelmed business owner into a much happier one.

Reduced Overheads

Many entrepreneurs do not have a fixed office address, but rely heavily on technology to keep them in touch. One of the main reasons for office premises is to house staff. If much of the tasks are carried out by external experts/providers, the need for premises is reduced if not eliminated.

It stuck in my mind when a few years ago at a conference, Social Media pioneer Penny Power said that her company – Ecademy - did not have a main office. Neither did she employ the senior members of her team; they were business people in their own right, who she chose to work with because of their expertise in their respective fields. Now as the years have gone by this may or may not still be the case at Ecademy. What it did show however; was that you could be efficient, effective and productive by concentrating on what needs to be done and eliminate unnecessary overheads and expenses.

More Time to Earn Money

Imagine how wonderful it would be to get up each day and know that your role in your business is to concentrate on the areas that you either enjoy the most and or feel are best suited to your talents; knowing that as important as the other areas are, they are being taken care of better than you ever could.

Well that is what entrepreneurs are able to do.

Because they are able to focus on the areas they are personally knowledgeable in, the business has a much greater chance to thrive.

Marketing and Sales, Financial Management, Product Development, Customer Service and Fulfilment are common to all business types in one form or another. In sole traders and grafter businesses these functions are dealt with by one or a few key people who are in danger of becoming frustrated because they are forced to perform functions that they are not the best equipped to carry out.

If for example you hate selling, then you need to bring in the expertise to take care of it.

Even Social media which has opened up the world to small entrepreneurs is not something that everyone in business embraces, even if they can see the benefits. There are companies out there that will do it for you.

Even though I am very sociable in the real world, and I could understand the plus side of social media, it was something I just did not have time to delve into because I was too busy being a jack of all trades. I saw it as a distraction rather than part of business development.

Once I had shifted some of my more repetitive tasks from my desk I found I had space to take it on. Now I still have a way to go in that area but I no longer feel as if I am stealing time, I got rid of the things I did not want to do so I could be freer to do what I choose.

The other main area is of course my baby; the bookkeeping and accounting side of the business. For many of my clients, it is their first journey into outsourcing a key part of their company. It is a revelation that now there are even one man bands working from home who have decided they will not use precious income generating time to record financial paperwork, but recognise the importance of keeping track of the money.

Some owners may have attempted to do it before, but had bad experiences; or they themselves did not keep to their side of the agreement to ensure the relationship went smoothly. Previously, despite the systems I have in place, I would have a few clients who provided 3 months worth of paperwork the week before they have a VAT Return due. They would then panic that they were going to get a fine.

So the trick is to choose a provider that has procedures and steps in place to make the transition as smooth as possible for you, and even within this initial bedding in period, you should quickly be able to see the advantages of offloading a task.

The number of tasks that can be passed to an outside professional is extensive and includes:

Bookkeeping (obviously), Social Media, IT support, copywriting, administration, email marketing, telephone answering, graphic design and web design.

Manage Costs

The beauty of using outside resources is that you can enlist them when you have an increase in demand for their services and reduce it as demand goes down or maybe funds become tight.

You can also use a provider to cover one-off projects so you can build them into your quotes and ensure you cover your costs and still make a profit.

Even though my product packages are based on an ongoing relationship, there is no minimum contract or tie-ins, so in theory if any of my clients wanted to take the bookkeeping back at any time they could. However I am pleased to say, even when they do cut back on supplier spending, our products tend to be the one of the ones they hang onto.

I prefer to believe it is totally a reflection of the wonderful service they receive, but the reality is we provide an alternative to one of the business owners' least favourite tasks and the desire to avoid it can be quite strong. Few entrepreneurs are as interested in the detail involved in the recording and reporting of finances, they just want an end result.

Build Foundation Ready for Growth

Many solopreneurs and grafter business owners do actually have sound plans in place to grow but are unable to do so because they can only do as much as they can personally fit into a day, week or month. They may not have sufficient expertise to expand the services beyond the initial offering; or they cannot source finance to fund the resources they need to expand.

By looking to outside expertise, whether as a supplier or partner, they can build a team from people that are ready to go, who are already experienced in what they want to do and this opens up the possibility of going after business that previously was beyond their capabilities with greater confidence.

Many of these experts would be very costly to bring on as employees and there is the danger of not being able to keep them occupied full time, so you end up with a costly overhead that is draining rather than earning you money.

Compete with Larger Competitors

You have a support team in place and you are now able to concentrate on your area of expertise. Competitors, who you felt were ahead of you, may no longer seem as formidable as you position yourself to achieve. With a business model of using resources as needed and keeping overheads low, you may well find you are more responsive to the customer needs than they are.

CHAPTER 4

Controlling the Control Freak

Growth is not always about size

May I take the opportunity to re-state the message of this book? It is about how we get real, how we are honest about ourselves and our business.

Are you insisting you have no plans to grow because you really do not welcome progression? If this is genuinely what you want and you are happy with where your business is right now, then you have already achieved what the rest of us fight so hard for - satisfaction within your own circumstances.

If however on reflection you now think this is not the case, what made you believe it was before? In my more personal conversations with business people, a common thread has been the frustration with their ability to move forward.

If this resonates with you, it may be that somewhere along the line, the enjoyment has waned, and the reason you started the business may no longer be incentive enough to keep you motivated.

Are you in a rut and just coasting borne of disillusionment? Is the decision to tick along a way to avoid feeling as though you have failed to accomplish your original goals?

Those whose original intention was to create a vehicle to fund a hobby or a less stressful way of life may not have this dilemma, because they never wanted to be in business in the true meaning. But if running your own flourishing enterprise and all that that entails has always been the objective and it has not happened, and of course deep inside it is what you really want; then look in the mirror and admit it.

If this is not an issue for you, then I hope the book can still help by showing all the options to make your life easier nonetheless. If this is however a sentiment you can relate to, then let us deal with it together.

My way to deal with such disharmony is to get things done. Action makes me feel better. I will be the first to admit that it has not always been the best course to take in all situations; but my greatest source of gloominess is not having a direction or plan of action. Once I do, I immediately feel more in control. But I totally respect the need to perhaps dig a little deeper into ourselves and address any issues that seem to hinder us personally, and you will more than likely find these issues impact on other areas of your life, not just work.

In my early years I was a real sceptic of self-help "gurus" and self improvement materials, but I was always open to the talking therapies. I think because, again, they required some participation on the part of the user of the service (the doing side of me). However, you have to react in a way that works for you.

As interesting and enlightening as I found have the high profile experts such as Anthony Robbins, Brian Tracy, Deepak Chopra, Rhonda Byrne et all, I was always more drawn to the 'how' in their messages rather than the 'why'. The 'why' fired me up but the' how' got me doing.

As I recall many a conversation that begun on a financial basis that eventually ended up going down a more personal or even emotional path, the underlying feelings and beliefs about ourselves and our abilities that hold us back are difficult to ignore, despite what our heads say.

I have already talked about Suzie in my list of amazing people at the beginning of the book. But in case you skipped it.

Someone who has had quite an impact on me is Suzie Greaves. She is a respected author, journalist, columnist and health editor for glossies such as OK Magazine and New Woman and Psychologies Magazine. She has navigated her way successfully through many of the challenges of life, relationships and business, and founded The Big Leap Coaching Company. She was very positive about my writing this book and sent me a message that gave me a great boost when I needed it. You can visit her site or contact her at http://www.suzygreaves.com

Some years ago, she and colleague, Carole Ann Rice, had a mini- workbook featured in a well known mainstream magazine article. I decided to put my scepticism aside and go through the questions. I shocked myself at some of the answers I gave. Knowing that what I wrote was for my eyes only allowed me to be totally honest. It was quite liberating; and the bit that stuck out for me was listing the things in my life that I was tolerating that I actually resented.

The article was called 7 Questions That Got Me the Life I Wanted.

If you search online or contact Suzie you can download an eBook version. It is easy to follow with each question explained and examples to help you with your answers and lots of space for you to make notes.

It targets your life as a whole, but you can relate it entirely to your business if you like, but it may surprise how closely entwined your personal and your business life frustrations are.

Below are the abbreviated versions of the questions:

1. What is the thing that makes you most afraid in your life and what are you going to do about it?

2. What do you need to do differently to create a reserve (more than enough) in 5 areas of your life?

3. What are the top 20 things or who are the people draining your energy from you and what do you have to do to eliminate them

from your life forever?

4. What are the top 20 things or who are the people who boost your energy and what do you have to do to change to get more of them in your life?

5. If you were brave, what 20 things might you do differently on a daily basis?

6. What would you have to believe to lead the life you always wanted and list 20 ways you can start "acting as if" you are?

7. It is five years from now. A journalist from your favourite newspaper/magazine is coming to interview you. What does your life look like now?

It is the type of exercise that requires you to disappear to a coffee shop or hotel for a night with lots of wine or copious amounts of coffee and work through it.

Treat it as a positive experience because the point is to come out with added energy to make progress. The first time I did this I confess I was quite depressed. It is tough to confront your disappointments - make no mistake, but unless you know what you are dealing with, how can you tackle them effectively?

Similarly with new clients that have been experiencing financial pressures, progress was frequently hindered due to avoidance of issues. Being able to quantify their situation provided a starting point for making changes.

Once we got on the case and systemised their financial records they were able to see exactly where they were. Worryingly their situations were often worse than they thought, because fear and procrastination had kept them from tackling their circumstances before.

Upstairs Not Downstairs

Lady Bellamy or Mrs Bridges? For those of you too young to remember Upstairs Downstairs, it was the Downton Abbey of its day. Both programmes show how belief systems and financial standing can totally dominate what you expect from life. Even if you dream of achieving great things, these factors have a profound effect on our behaviour. .

You have the responsibility of one who resides upstairs while also carrying the workload of the one who belongs downstairs.

Here you are calling yourself a business owner, but chances are you pay yourself less than the gardener you had when you had a job. You miss out on opportunities to network; meet collaborators and potential customers, because you are too busy. But all this being busy is not resulting in you earning any more money for you or for your family; or even if it is, you are too knackered to enjoy any of it.

When you entered those business cards onto your customer relationship database after your networking meeting the other day; what else could you have been doing? What! You haven't entered them onto your database because you haven't had time? But those were warm contacts who may well have remembered you if you touched base or followed up.

That nice virtual assistant that you met over coffee would have had that done. A good one may even have put together a mini email marketing campaign for you to keep in touch on a regular basis; and only requiring you to approve the content.

Now admittedly that is rich coming from me, because historically I have always wanted to learn how to do everything myself. I thrive on new skills and knowledge, in fact I can be quite a nerd, but it is a state of affairs I have had to get over. If it is not part of my core set of skills or requires me to split myself into even more parts then I put it on my "find someone who can" list.

Replicating Yourself

"Others won't do it as well as me"

If things are going in the right direction there will come a time when even the core skills that were unique to you will themselves become a hindrance. You will be required to remove yourself even further away from the day to day processes or run the risk of stifling any further progress.

One of the ironies of outsourcing; is that it is often the very decision to do it that pushes some businesses into considering adding to their internal personnel also. This may still be someone who is technically self-employed or in the case of lawyers and accountants, surveyors and other such professionals, it may mean taking on a partner.

This can be a real stumbling block for many, even those that have been working successfully with other providers. Now they need to share not just work and projects but often physical space. It is often the catalyst that persuades an entrepreneur to make the transition from home business to office based business. For those who really do not want the traditional office or do not want to be responsible for the day to day welfare of staff outsourcing provides a very real solution. In addition, technology has made the virtual office a very real alternative to the traditional bricks and mortar place of work.

Assuming your initial steps into outsourcing have resulted in your being able to extricate yourself somewhat from being mainly a worker; the odds are you are still doing most if not all of the "managing". So even though you may not be doing all the donkey work, you are still needed to make most of the daily decisions. Now I know that much decision making depends on your type of business and how staff intensive it needs to be. Whether it is a service or product based enterprise.

Businesses that sell products online will have more resource requirements than a photographer. The owner may have moved away from packing and labelling the products themselves to dealing with complaints and larger clients only. Nevertheless, they are still not devoting the necessary time to business development and achieving the freedom they desire.

Step forward their replacement. This may be in the form of a manager or a super- duper assistant but what about the advantages of a distribution provider who already has the mechanisms and resources needed to get your products to your customers in place? Being a broker and also affiliate selling is based on this very principle.

Moving up the ladder of your business is your aim, if you do not think you are eligible for promotion, who will?

Richard Branson is constantly sited as a genius at replicating himself in business. As accomplished and uber successful as he is; it is not beyond the range of us mere mortals, to do the same. It is the test of our resolve to let go. By this stage, you have hopefully experienced enough positive changes to not need too much of a push. The underlying challenge with this is moving away from tasks or responsibilities that to-date you have been protective of.

This could be paying bills, banking cheques, answering emails to senior clients/customers, dealing with queries, liaising with external providers.

Remember that new blood means new ideas, new techniques and renewed energy.

I remember having a big discussion with a fellow director a few years ago when I suggested he allowed someone else to open the post because it distracted him from the "to dos" he had for that day. It was his way of still feeling in control, as small as it was.

Be aware, your manager or super assistant still does not have to be a full-time employee, they could be part-time, or guess what... you guessed it, an external person, company or partner. You could partner with someone

in the same business as you who clearly wants to do the day-to-day managing while you prefer the innovative side, or vice versa.

The trick is to treat the relationship as a partnership so that it is a win-
win situation for all parties concerned. Money is usually not the only
reason for wanting to work alongside another person or company.

There was an episode of Dragon's Den when all five dragons made an
offer to a pair of entrepreneurs because they were creating a way of ensuring poor people in developing countries like Africa had access to
clean water when they needed it. It was as if the return on their investments was a distant second to the need to be part of something that ap-
pealed to them on a personal level. Despite how rich and successful they
are, they are still human beings with the same emotional triggers as other
people. Often the more successful a person is, the more in touch they are
with these triggers because they are no longer constantly focussed on
financial survival.

People with a continual lack of money focus more on themselves. I don't
mean this in a bad way, it is just that having to constantly watch the pen-
nies and juggling responsibilities are a matter of basic survival for people
in this position. Dealing with this is a priority on a day-to-day basis. This
is not the case for the rich; so they are mentally and emotionally freer to
give not just money, but time and effort to the needs of others. I believe
it is not the abundance of money that makes them more generous, but the
freedom that having money gives them to indulge their already present
desire to give.

Many were like this before they became rich; having money just means
they can do more for others than was possible before.

With few exceptions it is unlikely that you invented your area of expertise, so we can be safe in the assumption that you are not the only person
who can do what you do.

As an old colleague of mine used to say all the time "Get over yourself"

Once you do; you can leave the things behind that drain you; and enjoy the wealth of choice that it brings to your world; personally and professionally. I would go even further and suggest that you actively seek out not only people who can do what you do as well as you, but who can do it even better.

I Can't Afford It

Cost is possibly the biggest barrier against getting external help that entrepreneurs face. Now despite being an advocate of letting go, I do not ignore the fact that there are some practicalities that need to be in place.

When starting up a new business, particularly as a sole trader, the main concern is just getting enough business to cover costs. There probably is not enough activity to justify farming out tasks ad hoc, let alone on a regular basis. Even if there is, there may not be sufficient income to cover paying out

But the danger is we set up our businesses in such a way that even when things do improve financially, the structure of the business does not enable us to make the transition from relying on ourselves to do everything rather than sharing the load.

Even if at this point there is insufficient money coming into your business; you can still prepare for the day when you start building your team. This might be external or otherwise. The value of setting up your systems, procedures, guidelines etc all ready to support your future plans cannot be stressed enough. It is very tempting to delegate first and then work out the details later, resulting in an unsatisfactory result for all concerned.

The Income V Overwhelm Struggle

There you are, you have been trading for a while, and enough money comes in to pay your bills. You are good at what you do and you have a steady stream of work. This may not be from new business, but each month you get paid. The trouble is you are working around the clock. You are getting fed up and the tasks never seem to be finished.

You think back to when you started and you could barely make ends meet, to now when things are much better money-wise but you are overwhelmed by your workload.

The thought of someone else taking care of some of your tasks would be a dream come true and you even go as far as to investigate what your options would be, only to come to the conclusion there is not enough funds to cover taking this route as it would "take the food out of your mouth". The pain of robbing Peter to pay Paul is not forgotten and you have no desire to return to those times. So what do you do?

You resolve to work even harder to make even more money and then you will have the additional revenue you need to cover the cost of getting help. This will mean you are able to take time off here and there and so you can finally get that quality time with your family that you so desperately crave. However for many the fear of losing part of your income is greater than the fear of being overwhelmed by the tasks at hand.

"You just have to move faster and find more energy". You tell yourself. Phrases like work smarter not harder and work on the business not in it become mantras, but the behaviour just carries on as before. Only the months keep flying by and you may even have increased your income, but you are working even longer hours than you were before, and the regular quality time with your family still has not happened yet. In fact see you less of them than you did before. Even when you are in their company, mentally you are absent.

Those looks of impatience from your other half that says, "It is one thing that we don't see much of you, but we cannot even see the benefit. We are no better off than before, in fact we are worse off than when you had a job."

These are not incentives to go home on time even if you were able to.

Now let's not run away with the belief that successful entrepreneurs do not work ridiculously long hours also, but for them it is a choice. When they have down time it really is down time because they are secure in the knowledge that the business can continue without them. They are still earning money in their absence and any issues are being effectively dealt with.

Don't be fooled by the business people who convince themselves that their situation is the same just because they are able to leave the business for a period of time. Only to come back from time away to an almighty mess that will take them longer than the period of time they were away to clear up.

An industry that you may have guessed I am extremely familiar with – Accounting - ironically harbours some of the most devoted opponents of letting go.

Picture the scenario. It is the January Self-Assessment period which is one of the busiest times in the accounting/tax calendar.

We have Mr. or Ms. Accountant that studied for years and years to achieve some of the most demanding qualifications in the world; spending time sifting through little receipts thrown into a plastic bag or the famous shoe box; from a client who turns up at the last minute having either done no bookkeeping, or it is so poor it is of little use to complete their Tax Return. Mr. or Ms. Accountant may even be part of a group practice so the paperwork ends up being given to one of the other 'qualified' accountants. What a waste of their talent.

Imagine that this particular accountant charged their time at £70 per hour. How many other tax returns could have been done in that time? A competent admin person brought in just for January to cover this busy period at say £15 per hour would have done the job and not only saved Mr. or Ms. Accountant £55 per hour. It would have allowed them to use that same amount of time to generate extra income doing the work that makes them real money. The work that is best suited to their skills and which adds value to their clients. Instead they are throwing that money away sorting out fuel receipts and meals out that the client probably cannot claim for anyway.

The number of accounting/tax experts that take on regular bookkeeping instead of concentrating on offering more of their specialism is staggering. It is this very need to control that poses the greatest threat to achieving the freedom they crave. In many, not all cases, by any means can again be greater than the desire for freedom. In fairness the situation often comes about as they see that doing the work themselves is less painful than dealing with the muddle they will end up with afterwards, if they relied on someone else to do it.

Even if you do not sell your time for money, by charging hourly rates, there is a cost attached to your time regardless. Using that time on non-money making or business development tasks is costing, even if it is not tangible to you.

Non Financial Costs Of Doing It All

The financial consequences of overwhelm are obvious and very real to many. They include poor accounting/bookkeeping records leading to inaccurate data for management or owners to work with, late year end accounts, tax penalties and fines, poor cash flow, etc.

Apart from the impact on company money, the detriment such pressure has on physical, mental and emotional well- being cannot be overestimated. The slump in the shoulders of people that I meet during some of the reviews that I do is plain to see. Even more perturbing is the attempt, even at that stage, to show bravado and assure me or them, that all is under control and that the review is merely an exercise to see where they are.

Once they realise it is ok to be honest, the whole tone of the meeting changes and then at the end we usually end up laughing. The realisation that one is not alone; and they are not the only person that feels as they do, can be so cathartic in itself.

In the world of employment it can be quite easy to spot staff that are feeling overwhelming pressure. More time off sick, work that was previously up to scratch deteriorating, or silly mistakes made, it becomes difficult to manage them.

The same symptoms affect us as self-employed and small business owners, but we seem to feel less inclined to acknowledge they exist, let alone confront and deal with them. At least in the workplace, they may have other workers to share concerns with, even if it was just a quick moan during coffee break. When you work alone or are in charge alone, this is not so easy. How many of you have stopped telling your husbands, wives or friends about your day for fear of sounding too negative? Have you experienced the roll of the eyes that says, "Here we go again"? Or have you not even gotten that far because you don't want to admit that all is not as it should be?

Whether real or perceived, if an undercurrent of dissatisfaction with your business has become a constant, you need to resolve it because it will spill over and poison your physical and emotional fitness.

As a person who suffers from high blood pressure, allowing such pressures to engulf me is not an option as the consequences are dire. Having been through the fire and back, I cannot stress enough the rewards that are possible by taking the bull by the horns and making your health and wellbeing a number one priority.

I have met many business owners who are in the position others would like to be, yet they feel unfulfilled. The grass does commonly seem greener on the other side as they say. For so many of us when we started out and had no customers or work, the thought of being busy was a dream. Then we made sales, became busy and the thought of being less busy but still able to earn money became the dream. We have goals or milestones and as we arrive at them, the goals and milestones change and move. The point is we never really arrive; we just keep travelling hopefully through more and more interesting experiences. If this is the case we had better make sure that the journey is one that will contribute positively to our lives, otherwise what is the point.

Try this little exercise:

Take the time to stop and look back at your business timeline. Remember what it was like when you started out? Did you have a lot of money to play with? Did you have any customers? Did you have a website? If you did have a website, was it the best it could be for your business? Was your computer up to date with all the software that you needed? Was your logo and branding sorted? Did you have accurate and up-to-date accounting records or forecasts? Did you have comprehensive profiles on the main Social Media sites? Add any more you can think of.

____

____

____

The chances are you would have answered no to many; if not all of the questions above.

Now answer the same questions but fast forward to the present day. While you may not have everything as you would like; see how many things you have achieved that you had not even started in the beginning.

____

____

____

____

Even if you are not at what you consider one of your milestones, you may surprise yourself at just how far you have come. Celebrate your efforts. Take the energy from that and now focus on where you are headed; now that you have more weapons in your arsenal. Look at how much you did with - in many cases – some knowledge and a whole lot of blind enthusiasm. Just imagine what you can do now you have additional knowledge, a wealth of experience and that enthusiasm you had before, just not so blind this time.

START HERE

CHAPTER 5

Planning Your Freedom

If you are feeling oppressed by the responsibilities of your business and you do not have the luxury of trained, productive staff at your disposal. There are two things that will have a profound effect on your relationship with your company. One is understanding and streamlining your finances. The other is effective use of outsource providers. This is your opportunity to stretch your entrepreneurial muscle by exhibiting one of the cornerstones of the true entrepreneur, delegation and team building.

Deciding What to Outsource

The idea of handing tasks to others to create more time is attractive to most of us, but when it comes to actually doing it, can cause us much anxiety. One of the main reasons being; not knowing how to go about it.

What do I need?

Why not try this exercise?

Create a list of the roles and tasks that you perform in your business and then note which ones:

1. Make you feel stressed by the thought of tackling them

2. Take up a lot of your time but do not move your business forward

3. Are repetitive, and if you were honest, are not the best use for your talents, but needs to be done

4. Requires you to learn a new skill or improve an existing skill that is not going to be carried out by you personally long term, well, not if you have your way

5. And also crucially make note of what I call the R.I.P tasks. How many things do you do that just plain and simply do not really need doing? Borne of habit or because "It is always the way you have done it" Can they be dumped altogether?

Two tasks that I laid to rest were: Excel forms called the Sales List and Purchases List. They were printable tables showing the breakdown of the client's sales invoices or purchase invoices depending on which list of course. They showed the date, customer name, price and VAT, the date paid, method of payment and some other bits of information. They were a throw back to my paper-based accounting days and I had a few accountants that quite liked them so they would get a copy periodically. For clients with lots of transactions it was time consuming to complete and I realised that I rarely referred to them myself. The main reason I did it was to keep my accountant colleagues happy. It certainly did not enhance my service to my clients either.

Plus here was I setting up computerised systems for others yet hanging onto a manual task purely out of habit. One day the obvious hit me. If the client data was being entered correctly into the computerised system, always keeping in mind the type of reports that are required at the other end, I would be able to pull out the same information at the touch of a button.

Do you have any tasks like this? They are often found lurking in the repetitive tasks list of items, protected by the cloak of familiarity.

Now that you have done your first list – you will see that as your business grows, the mix of tasks will evolve and will need to be reviewed. You may have realised as you jotted things down that some of the items you identified as not being needed, had survived not just for practical reasons but also due to personal or emotional ones. The first time I did not complete a sales list for a client, I was convinced there would be some disaster and it would all have been avoided if I had left things as they were. Needless to say, as time has gone on, I am more irritated by how long I waited before ditching them.

Do not disregard your intuitive feelings about a task. For example if you hate dealing with paper, you hate dealing with paper, and no matter how much your head tells you it is important, it is likely to end up being left until it cannot be avoided any longer. At this point, it will potentially not be completed satisfactorily because it is now about catching up.

Allow your true feelings about a task to be aired, even if you just acknowledge it to yourself. One of the greatest rewards of running the business you want is having the freedom to do the roles and tasks that please you. You work hard; you deserve to be happy doing it.

Who do I need?

Now I am going to give you the same exercise but with a different emphasis. You have explored WHAT you can outsource as a yardstick for choosing your tasks and roles. Now I ask you to do the same exercise again, but this time, explore WHO you can outsource to.

If you are a networker particularly if you are a member of a structured networking group such as BNI, 4 Networking, Athena etc or you work with a masterminding group you certainly have a list of WHO's that you know personally and have experience of their talents either first or second hand.

1. Who do you meet with or network with that you know could help you but you dismiss because you think you cannot afford it?

2. What tasks or areas of your business are you struggling with that you cannot seem to resolve satisfactorily; despite knowing just the person who could handle it with ease?

3. Who do you know that uses outsourced providers regularly or as an essential part of their venture? What are their experiences and who do they recommend?

4. Do you know a:

- Web designer
- Copywriter
- Graphic designer
- Social Media expert
- IT support person or company
- Recruitment consultant
- Virtual admin assistant
- Telephone answering service
- Bookkeeping service
- Sales person
- Research company
- PR expert
- Marketing consultant
- Human Resources and employment expert
- Credit Control service
- Distribution and Delivery company

And this is only a snapshot of expertise that you can tap into.

Clarifying Your Requirements to an Outsource Provider

Before we go any further, may I reiterate that while I am focusing primarily on dealing with delegating non-core tasks, some of the examples I will share with you include core tasks, because that is the area that needs to be delegated for some. Nevertheless, as you will see in some of the examples, the same basic principles will still apply whether they are core tasks or not. Some businesses can outsource core tasks easier than others depending on the nature of the work, the complexity and the availability of appropriate suppliers.

When I was worked in IT in the City I had a very profitable client that was a company started by a man who had an idea for creating a large IT rental organisation. He found other people to cover every role in the organization. Admittedly he employed most of them, but what I found fascinating about him, was that although he was the brains, he had no desire to do anything but work in the accounts department.

This was a dynamic sales orientated company and people never realised that the heart of the company was a man who faxed them their monthly statements – yes I said fax, it was a long time ago. He was apparently extremely shy and did not feel comfortable being a front man. Not to mention, in accounts, he could keep a constant eye on the numbers as that is what floated his boat.

More often than not however, the considerations of outsourcing your core business require concentrated in-depth preparation because you are dealing with the areas that make up your very livelihood. The scope involved in that requires greater dedication to the subject than I will go into in this book.

As I stated before, not everything should necessarily be done externally. You may decide that you will always employ staff for certain jobs, particularly if you are looking at who can take over from you as your role within the business progresses. This could be in terms of doing the technical/knowledge based work, taking on the managerial aspects or who you would like to take the overall reigns if and when you decide you no longer want to.

You may decide that you want to retain ownership and get an income but stay out the day-to-day running of the business. Alternatively you may want to sell outright and you recognize that the less dependent on you, the business is, the more attractive it is to other potential buyers and the more money you can command. Again this is a large subject. I highly recommend the book "Built to Sell" by John Warrillow which is about how his journey from owner/manager to business owner helped his business become more sellable.

What Roles Do I Need To Fill?

We have looked at examples of activities that you can pass on to others. That list is just the tip of the iceberg. With that list mind, let us explore how you can relate them to your own company.

If you have done a business plan of some description, the odds are you would have produced an organisation chart. Standard charts are often based on the organisation as it stands, i.e. you are merely drawing up a diagram of the people you currently have and what they do. For a sole trader that is commonly one box with their name and all the jobs listed below. If you are already experiencing overwhelm, seeing that laid out could be all you need to tip you over the edge; which could be one reason conventional solopreneurs don't bother to do one.

Produce an organisation chart based on the actual roles, tasks and jobs that need to be carried out. Forget who you have in your company and if it is only you, ignore this fact also. What you are trying to establish are the functions that are required to achieve your business aims. What are the various areas that form the foundations of your business?

When I did this the first time, I split mine into Innovation tasks, Sales and Marketing tasks, Internal tasks and Financial tasks. Though these heading still form the basis of my main chart to some degree, as time has moved some of the headings have been amended and others added.

The most important thing to remember when you do this exercise is that there are no walls or limits. Do not let the limitations of your current situation or any negative feelings you may have narrow your vision. This is about moving forward, shaking things up.

You may only for example be using social media and doing the odd bit of networking because they are in your comfort zone and budget, but if you know that what would drive your sales is an experienced sales person or team then put it down.

If packaging and sending your orders out to customers is taking up too much time or you have run out of space, imagine the possibility of having a fulfilment company do it for you.

If you are constantly diverting your landline to your mobile and calls go to voicemail, how much of an improvement would a call answering service be?

Nothing is out of your reach with this project. Have fun with it, think big, be creative and be bold. If you cannot do it on paper, how will you do it in reality?

This is a framework for positive change and as you evolve so will your chart. Formalise to realise it as they say.

Filling the Roles

Now you have your organisation chart, the next step is to fill in roles and tasks with real people. If you have done this diligently a number of things will become apparent:

1. The obvious one is you are probably placed in too many boxes and cannot possibly be expected to do all these jobs equally well

2. There are roles and tasks that you did not realise you needed or conversely you thought you needed but do not add value or support your business goals.

3. You have roles and tasks that you have wanted to fill for some time but have not got around to sorting out. This could be due to time and money restraints, or a lack of information about how or who would be best, etc.

4. Possibly the most contentious, where you already have staff or suppliers currently fulfilling certain roles and tasks, but these are not the right choices. In an ideal world you would not have them in that position.

And that conclusion includes you.

Partner, Associate, Sub-contractor or Supplier?

Now while the terms above are used interchangeably, I will give you my take on them and why they have totally different definitions in my mind. And depending on which one is required, how it can totally change your approach to fulfilling a role.

When I talk about a partnership I am not just discussing the standard partnership where two or more people; who would otherwise be sole traders come together to form one legal entity. As in the case of many professional set-ups like legal firms and accountancy practices.

Partnership in this context also encompasses two or more individuals or companies who form partnerships based on a common business aim. It may only relate to one area of their businesses and the parties could still remain separate sole traders or companies.

The need to widen or expand the range of products or services is a common reason for smaller concerns to contemplate following this path. A car mechanic who is always getting requests for body work repairs may decide to partner with a body shop to offer a one-stop repair service. A will writer and probate expert may partner with a financial advisor to form a more extensive financial planning business than they could provide singularly.

Because of the formal nature of these agreements, the wise should always take legal advice regarding the terms of the partnership. Not least because of the dependency of each person or company on the other. If you are acting as a partnership you may now actively market, whether separately or jointly, the products and services of both companies rather than just providing them if and when asked.

It is imperative that both parties feel they are in a win-win position to ensure they keep up their end of the contract. In a traditional partnership the emphasis is more on the legal and financial responsibilities of the parties because everyone is part of one organisation and so automatically "on the same side". But in a partnership where the actual businesses remain separate, the overriding loyalty will always be to their own business. So being sure you are dealing with people of integrity, and that all terms are clear, agreed and workable is just touching on what you need to take into account.

I will not go into the advantages and disadvantages as that could be a book in itself and there is comprehensive information all over the Internet.

The scenarios are endless. Imagine that person A cannot afford to employ or pay the rates or fees of person B, but wants to utilise their skill or expertise as could be the case with our car mechanic mentioned above. That is not to say that car mechanics cannot make enough money to pay for personnel but just humour me for the purposes of illustration. If the car mechanic was given a choice and decided that they would rather offer the service themselves but sees the partnership as the only viable option at present, or even "a necessary evil" then the attitude to the relationship may already be starting off on the wrong foot. The advantages to both parties must be at the heart of any agreement.

Suppose person C has an idea but does not have the necessary experience to make it a reality so they partner with person D who does. The innovator meets the implementer. As long as each is doing what they see as their strength then this can be very fruitful.

Even more commonplace is person E who has the idea, knowledge, experience and teams up with person F who has the money.

Many years ago when I still in the world of employment, I knew a couple of not so young men in the music business. One had a little black book of music contacts and the other was in his element nurturing raw singing talent. They resolved to join forces and form an artist management service. Now the talent and skills of both is not in question. The one with the contacts had a natural flair for building relationships and attracting interested people, and the other had a method to systematically coach a singer/performer to get them to improve.

So what got in the way?

Well for one, they spent lots of time, money and energy getting the terms and agreements done that related to their clients/artists, but there was nothing outlining the relationship between the two of them. It had not really been discussed verbally let alone formalised. Because they were friends most things were implied but not specified.

As the work began on their first few artists it became obvious that the majority of the work was being done by Mr. Method, even tasks that didn't naturally fall into his remit. He was the implementer of the two and very much into working to deadlines. Mr. Black Book had very little concept of time but understood that the nature of some music people was not based on dates and times, but that quality of the output was the goal and if it took 3 times as long then so be it.

Mr. Method was getting frustrated at the speed at which money was being spent while Mr. Black Book saw it as a natural part of the industry and that they would get in back in spades when their artist was signed.

Now those differences in themselves often are the things that make the partnership work because the meeting of the two types of people form a whole. Sometimes you need to be cautious, other times you need to take risks. The irony with these two was that the breakdown came because Mr. Method became increasingly fed up with the workload as it seemed to him that Mr. Black Book was just socialising, turning up at rehearsals for updates and going off again.

In a conversation with him, I pointed out that just like in intimate relationships; the very thing that attracted you to the person initially is often the very thing that drives you crazy as time goes by.

Lover boy's socks on the floor in the early days are cute; after 2 years of marriage it is untidy and gets on your nerves. The same action, different stage of the relationship. Mr. Method and Mr. Black Book had never properly thought through, let alone addressed, what the actual business tasks and roles would be, or who would be responsible for what and who would actually carry out what jobs.

It may be that equality in all areas was not realistic. Mr. Black Book clearly saw what he did as just as valuable as what Mr. Method did, but Mr. Method felt he did not pull his weight.

And by now the initial flush of enthusiasm was beginning to wane as the realities of running a business was getting in the way of the enjoyment.

I pointed out to Mr. Method that I doubted Mr. Black Book was deliberately avoiding doing things and that to give him the benefit of the doubt and work on the assumption he just does not realise what is needed.

"Have you talked to him about how you feel?" I asked, knowing the answer was no because he knew it would come out as irritability and did not want a confrontation or to fall out with his partner.

So I suggested a meeting between the two of them to discuss their company and what their future plans were. Basically, what they should have done at the beginning. He was to turn up with a list showing the roles and responsibilities of their organisation and together they were to fill in who was responsible for what role and who would do what task.

The idea was that they would be able to see in simple form what was required, where they were now in relation to those requirements and what they needed to do to fill any gaps. But more importantly the meeting would be based on positive development rather than airing grievances.

I spoke to Mr. Method a little while after their meeting and he thanked me for the suggestion and it turned out when they filled in the names against the tasks and roles, Mr. Black Book was quite shocked as to how much Mr. Method actually did and was really apologetic for not realising sooner.

Great stuff! However what the meeting did reveal was that the two had very different reasons for getting involved which affected the level of commitment that each could and wanted to give. Sufficiently different to lead them to the conclusion that they were never really going to be able to work together and that it was not worth jeopardising a lifelong friendship for.

I have no idea what their financial situation was like or if it was a viable business proposition. That was not the nature of my connection with them, but in their case they would eventually have hit trouble.

In the spirit of balance let us remember that when a partnership works, it really works. Who can dispute the successes of William Hewlett and Dave Packard, Sony and Ericsson, Richard Rogers and Oscar Hammerstein, Rolls Royce and Daimler, Union Bank of Switzerland (UBS) with S. G. Warburg & Co and Dillon Read & co which has morphed into the mighty UBS Investment Services (rogue traders aside).

There are industries that naturally lend themselves to partnering, such as weddings, travel, property and maintenance. Do not let over enthusiasm blind you to the pitfalls. Take the time and set things up properly.

Business Associate

Now this term, much like "Information Technology" covers a wide area and means different things to different people. I have a number of business associates and when I use the expression, I am referring to people or businesses with whom I do business to enable me to offer prospects, customers and clients more than I would be able to on my own.

We have no long-term agreement in place with regards to our actual business set-up as is the case with a partnership. My dealings with some are ongoing because client needs demand it, or on an ad hoc basis. I have business associates who are accountants with whom the relationship is constant because we have mutual clients. I also have dealings with insolvency practitioners on a case by case basis; usually if a company is restructuring, has gone into administration, ceased trading etc, and the owner/director is making a fresh start or implementing changes to avoid history repeating itself. They may well decide to stay away from doing the day-to-day accounting themselves and get the assistance of a professional.

I recently took on such a client. Apart from the worries of making and keeping the business profitable, they were now dealing with the added pressure of being accountable to outsiders. They were appointed a business coach who would meet with them on a monthly basis to analyse the accounts to spot any areas of concern before they escalate, and to plan future strategy, etc. This would have been impossible before because they just could not keep the book-keeping up to date with all the fire fighting.

The first meeting took place and we attended virtually. As it progressed, if any information was needed in addition to what they already had, we emailed it over to them immediately. The director telephoned me later to say thank you as it made both him and his manager look so professional. He said some of the reports he handed over to the business coach meant nothing to him but that fact that he had them to hand was brilliant.

(Note to self: must pin him down for a brief session on understanding his financial reports).

He is not unusual, I have other clients who have to be "persuaded" to look at the details as they are only interested in the bottom line and just want everything summarised. In fairness, there are only so many hours in the day after all.

Based on the information and the outcome of the management meetings, their accountant could be updated regularly, so any tax or compliance issues would be spotted in advance. The good accountants out there can also make excellent business advisors; more so, they are able to spend more time concentrating on interpreting and analysing your financial records instead of sorting it out.

The nature of these agreements differ, depending on who I am dealing with and whether I am the main contact to the client or if I am the associate in the background. With some, there is no agreement at all, just a mutual trust built up over time or due to recommendation by a trusted contact.

Though I remember when I started doing work for a well-respected accountancy practice in Canary Wharf being given a contract of at around 12 pages and in small fonts. I can only imagine what you would have to sign to become a real partner, they must insist on a share of your children.

We form associations as a natural part of networking. Networking organisations like BNI, 4 Networking Athena, etc, have been great advocates of using this form of relationship building to encourage businesses to support each other and to enhance their own reputations in the process.

They may involve monetary rewards from one to the other such as referral fees, preferential rates, sharing of sales or profits, etc.

Business associations can be the catalyst that leads to the forming of a formal partnership.

Sub-Contractor

I will talk about sub-contracting in its legal sense even though like partner or associate it is used in a variety of situations relating to the farming out of work.

Sub-contractors are traditionally found in industries such as construction, IT and other specialist trades. An individual sub-contractor straddles that fine line between employee and self-employment that can have tax and legal implications on the company/individual or contractor they carry out work for.

Sub-contractors very often go to the premises of the hirer to perform the work required, using the tools and resources provided. They may be told specifically what jobs, tasks, and roles to carry out. The hirer can be one of only a few if not their only source of income. Being in this position can give leverage to the tax man to deduce that despite what the sub-contractor may be called by the parties concerned, that they are in fact for the purposes of tax liabilities, employee.

In the UK labour law case Autoclenz v Belcher, self-employed sub-contracted workers took the hiring company (Autoclenz) to court. This was based on the argument that they were treated as employees in terms of how the work was allocated and expected to be carried out, but without the benefits.

It was not unusual to find individuals trading as limited companies because hiring companies did not want the headache of falling foul of the tax laws. Many organisations shied away from taking on self-employed sub-contractors for that reason. They would only entertain using their services if they were a legitimate Limited company, all be it with only one person.

The Construction Industry Scheme (CIS) is a tool used by the tax office supposedly to enable flexibility and transparency in this area, on the other hand it has brought with it additional paperwork, compliance and taxation for those who fall under its umbrella. It requires the hiring company "Contractor" to deduct a percentage at source from the invoice it receives from the sub-contractor and forward that directly to the tax office every month. At time of going to print, this is 20%.

As always, do your homework first so you understand the implications of sub-contracting and of being a contractor. Below are some links to sites with further information:

Work out if you are employed or self-employed:

www.direct.gov.uk/en/MoneyTaxAndBenefits/Taxes/WorkingAnd PayingTax/DG_4015975

What is CIS?

http://www.hmrc.gov.uk/cis/intro/whatis-cis.htm

If all that seems like a lot of work, start with a discussion with your accountant. Failing that contact us at Financial Gym or and we will put you in the hands of my CIS experts Andrew and Steve who would be happy to point you in the right direction.

Supplier

This is the method of outsourcing that is most familiar to small business owners. Of the four options I have covered, this can work out to be the most flexible of all; as it allows you to dip your toe in the water of delegation without getting your feet too wet.

We all deal with suppliers in one shape or form, but viewing suppliers as part of your team and capable of taking things off your plate so you don't have to do it can be quite a mind shift for some people. I am not just talking about those of you who want to delegate more tasks but do not know how, but also to those who do not see the point, or who consider it an extravagance or waste of money that their business cannot afford.

I accept start up businesses are usually not in the position to afford outside help in the early days. But even when money is coming in doing as many tasks as possible themselves is the goal, in the hope of keeping costs down..

To be honest, this is a trait that I myself possessed in my early days. But let us remember that it comes from a good place. We are brought up to value hard work and of taking responsibility and those are things to be proud of. Successful entrepreneurs do not give up hard work. It is just the areas in which the effort is directed that differs.

In my own experience I have found that with the possible exception of a web designer, for many of my clients, my business is often their first taste of outsourcing a non-core but critical element of their company for a long period of time. There may have been previous attempts that failed for one reason or another, so they are wary of going down the same road again, especially with something as private as their financial situation. By the time they are ready to work with me, I not only have to show the benefits of the particular products and services but reassure them that the process of letting go can work successfully.

The thought of not having to do the daily, weekly, monthly accounts is very appealing to the majority, but the thought of not having control over it can fill them with apprehension. As a rule I hold back from pointing out that they are probably not in control of it anyway, they are merely in possession of paperwork. Buying accounting and bookkeeping software is for many a false economy. Many believe that by possessing expensive software or monthly software subscriptions automatically means true understanding of the subject. Some of my best clients had very good software often set up and loaded. Only to then find that it had not been touched for months after they hit a stumbling block, hence my presence in their business.

I would initially set up and implement systems they get on with it themselves, but more often than not what they really wanted was to avoid doing it at all. So my business became more about making that process less daunting.

CHAPTER 6

Finding a Provider

Sourcing and implementing outsource providers is a topic that is a book in itself. Facilities and supply chain management are industries in themselves. You may be surprised to learn just how many functions plenty of large organisations do not carry out themselves.

Let us assume you have done the following:

You have thought about whom you know and what are skills are currently available to you in your existing contacts. This serves to open your mind, not just to the possibilities of collaborating and outsourcing but as to how close you are to skills, knowledge and experience that can enhance your business if you choose to take advantage of them.

Never mind six degrees of separation, you may be only one or two away from the people that will transform your working life.

You have created an organisation chart showing what roles and tasks are needed in your business even if it is just currently only you.

You have started to fill in the chart with actual people and companies who can fill those roles or carry out the required tasks.

The Desired Outcome

Be clear what the end result will be and identify what would constitute a successful outcome.

This may well be amended as you start to speak and negotiate with providers because you may discover services available to you that you were not aware of before. It may become apparent that your outcomes are unrealistic, particularly if your budget is limited. You could even find yourself revising your organisation chart because you discovered an element of your business that you could be free of that was not previously obvious. The best planning is rarely done alone anyway. Quality planning requires different personalities and skills that are seldom found in one person. This is the beauty of communicating outside of our businesses, it opens up a world of possibilities and opportunities that we would otherwise be unaware of.

Project or Task Statement

Describe the role, task or project in a statement that can be easily understood by potential providers. This will help you to target the right type of provider when you go searching. It could take some time before you find the right person or company and you do not want to be distracted by incompatible providers. If you decide to advertise, it will hopefully discourage providers who do not fit the profile from wasting your time and reduce any misunderstandings down the line.

For example a company that specifically wants outsourced bookkeeping may compose a statement that says:

"I require a supplier to complete my bookkeeping and provide me with a profit and loss report each month. They must be able to provide all the tools required including the software as I do not have the facility to provide office or desk space and will not be buying any software. They must be experienced with a recognised qualification and have procedures to make it easier for me to work with them as I do not know what I need to have or what I need to do. I will expect them to liaise with my accountant to get my year end company accounts completed."

It will make it clear in your own mind what you want when you do actually communicate with a provider so you can ask questions relevant to your situation. The statement above clearly states that you do not have desk space for another person, particularly if you work from home, and having a person in your house may not appeal. Many bookkeepers prefer to work at client premises because they themselves do not have the space to store files etc. In this case they would not be suitable.

If you are considering a provider for a customer service task, like fulfilling customer deliveries, or for a core role you may well have to supply a more comprehensive statement which may well form the basis for a full-blown role/task specification.

I would recommend the more crucial the role the more detailed you are about what you want.

Timescales

Is it for the completion of a one-off project?

I have a client that provides web hosting and web design services and the owner is an experienced web designer himself but frequently hires in external designers for one-off jobs. This is usually because they have superior expertise in a particular area of design. It is not unusual for a web expert to be a specialist in the actual design while another is a specialist in Search Engine Optimisation (SEO) and they both may work with a copywriter to get the readability of the site correct. Once a particular site is finished or the customer is happy, the relationships come to an end until the next project.

Is it for on-going support with a view to a long term relationship?

This tends to be the main reason people contact the Financial Gym and Precision Services. The financial records are like household bills, they just keep coming. It is the area of business that is often the most prevalent at eating into business development and money earning time for small businesses. Very few business owners do it well. Not to mention that the process of doing book-keeping and accounts holds little interest to most people. They just want the information that comes out at the other end. Worryingly even then it is too frequently just for the benefit of their accountant and HMRC, but I will cover that topic later on.

Accounting has often started off as one-off projects where Precision Services has been required to go into a business that has just recently bought Sage, QuickBooks, FreeAgent or some other accounting software. Armed with the technology and wanting to justify the money spent on software they are prepared to take care of it on a day to basis and only require help with setting up the system and some training. There are four main scenarios that shift the requirement from a single need to an ongoing one:

- The business continuously comes up against things that are not understood or things that they are unsure how to deal with, so require further training. They may constantly have questions or spend time that they do not have looking up answers and are still not confident they have got it right

- Done nothing or very little so have forgotten what they learned and the paperwork is piling up

- Know what to do, but is just not priority amongst the other daily pressures; so gets left until they can catch up.

- And my favourite reason: the owner has made a decision to concentrate on developing the business and needs accurate information regularly to make this happen. Crucially they consider bookkeeping not the best use of their skills and time

Standard Service or Bespoke

Do you have definite ideas of what you need? If so, the provider must work within that or do you want to have as little to do with the process as possible?

For example if you need your website done, do you only want someone to design it and then you have the ability to make minor changes yourself? Or will you require a fully managed web service where you inform the design team when you want to update it and they do it for you? Will it be an e-commerce site with a constantly changing inventory that requires monitoring? Will it be important for you to have the ability to make changes? These needs will limit which providers you can use.

What Level Of Communication Do You Want?

Do you require regular human contact, e.g. someone who you can meet with on a regular basis or will they be required to come to your premises periodically? Alternatively, is a virtual service more than enough for your needs? Do they need to be local or could they be based anywhere, even abroad?

Solo Provider or Team?

If you are looking for IT support, you may prefer to know there is a team of people so that you can get rapid response in an emergency, but if you are hiring a copywriter the fact they work alone is neither here nor there.

Are you concerned about how established, experienced or qualified they are?

What you do not want to be is a guinea pig client. However if you feel the risks are minimal; and you could even be offered some form of incentive or compensation for allowing yourself to be part of a trial or training process, then go ahead. It could end up being really cost effective if your desired results are achieved. Much like the way hairdressers give clients hair treatments at really low prices if they allow a trainee to do their hair.

For data entry work for example, you could use a student with spare time on their hands. My son is a Sage Accounting veteran and he doesn't even know it.

Selection Criteria

Examples include:

Prior knowledge of person or company

Qualifications:

- Track Record

- Location

- Personality

- Availability

- Lines and Forms of Communication

- Price

Buying on Price

Because money is the hinge that so much of your decisions will rest on, I thought it merited a mention of its own. Firstly, please do not base your decision to either explore outsourcing or who you eventually choose to work with based mainly on price. There is much to the saying "pay peanuts and get monkeys" but it is not as simple as that. By the same token paying over the odds also does not make sound business sense.

In Chapter Three – Step Back to Gain Control, I talked about the non-financial advantages of not having to do everything yourself. But let's be real, possibly the biggest obstacle to achieving this is the availability of money. Many entrepreneurs that I have dealt with are afraid of going down this route and then find they cannot continue to pay for the service and then would experience a sense of failure as a result, so they do not start at all.

I am not about to give you a magic bullet answer to that, because if one existed we would all have done it. But if you are looking at your business overall, there will be other red flags showing if you are not on top of your game. You may need to pure and simply focus on sales and marketing; and getting rid of none sales generating tasks has to be a priority.

When I first started using associates and external providers it certainly did affect my finances. But I had more time to network and sort out my after sales care process which up until that point had been on the fly. It helped to strengthen my relationships with my existing customers which in turn improved my income, because I was able to increase my prices without any objections.

Yes there will be a cost involved; and if you are a home business without staff it may well be in addition to other expenses. A company replacing full-time employees will see the cost saving immediately in a reduction in their fixed costs. I will avoid the issue of the ethics of laying people off for this reason because it is a decision that I believe no responsible business owner takes lightly, but in times of survival people must do what is necessary.

If you view the buying in of outside skills or labour as an investment in the development of your business and if you plan to measure what you will be able to achieve in terms of money, time and peace of mind, then the benefits will far outweigh the costs. One of my builder clients used to do their accounts at night when they returned from client sites. To be honest, he still can often be found working at night, but he is producing sales quotes instead. He has since added a credit control service to chase his outstanding invoices. The result is, he is no longer getting into difficult conversations with clients onsite about payment or lack of. Money aside, he just used to find it awkward and embarrassing and was glad to not have to do it anymore.

If your business is still in its infancy, then of course money is more likely to be tight and outsourcing is just not an option. Nonetheless I have worked with start-ups that made the decision to go down this route from day one. If however your business has been trading for some time, and your sales and profits are either not increasing, stagnating or even declining, then regardless of the finances, major changes have to made otherwise there will be no business let alone no money.

As stated earlier in the chapter, ensure than any agreement is a mutually beneficial one and you are both getting what you want. You need to feel you are getting a value for money service or skill and the provider is able to give you want you want at a rate that enables them to do the best job. If you go with the cheapest option the obvious risk is that the standard could be poor. They cannot meet deadlines consistently and you end up having to replace them. Meaning you could end up having to go through the search process all over again.

Also be aware that with the economic climate putting businesses under pressure, the temptation is to accept any work that comes along so a supplier may agree to meet your price just to get you on board because they need the income. Too often this means they have to cut corners or may not be as responsive to you as they would be to a more profitable client so you find yourself getting below average service. Or you get billed for things entitled "extras" frequently that you regarded as standard as they try to make up any shortfalls.

This is the very type of uncertainty your finances and development plans can do without.

Can They Provide References or Testimonials?

Who else has used them and what has been their experience of the service to-date? Can the provider give you case studies that relate to you and your situation?

Be prepared to understand and accept terms and conditions if applicable. Do not let the excitement of unloading a job, make you careless. Be sure you know what they will provide and that it meets your criteria and conversely, ensure that you are prepared to meet theirs. If there is an area you do not have absolutely clarity about or you are not totally comfortable with, raise it before any work begins.

What Provisions Do You Want To See Regarding Confidentiality And Non-Disclosure?

I provide my clients with a signed confidentiality agreement that cover me and my workers; in other relationships this part is often just implied. Because of the nature of my service I believe it is imperative that my clients feel they can trust us not to blab about their financial affairs. It can be enough of a leap for them to come to terms with my company seeing their finances, let alone anybody else.

Where to Find Providers

We have already touched on existing contacts as a source of skills but in addition there are:

- Networking contacts

- Referrals from other business contacts

- Research on line for particular requirement e.g.

- Online freelance agencies e.g.

  Elance.com and PeoplePerHour.com and other specialist providers

- Professional and trade bodies that represent the profession or trade you are looking for

- Temp/ recruitments agencies

- Social Media sites - such as LinkedIn, Facebook and Twitter.

Baby Steps First – Minimising Bad Outsourcing Experiences

- You have established what you need or what you struggle to take care of

- You know what results you expect from a provider

- You have found the person or company for the role or task

- You have agreed pricing and terms that suit you both

- You are now ready to begin the relationship.

I will confess that the mistake that I am about to describe is the one that tripped me up; because in my untrained mind, outsourcing just meant finding the person and handing everything over, oh how wrong I was.

In the early days I had, and still have my lovely, my lovely Gill who is an excellent bookkeeper. However she needed very flexible work days, so for very busy periods I would get in extra hands.

If I had a pound for every freelancer or temp that I used and would give tasks to, only to have to return to the mess that they had made, I would be on course to buy Trump Tower. I once had a "qualified" account temp that sat in my office for 6 hours and had only entered 20 items on the systems and every one of them was incorrect. Mercifully I always have backups so it was just a matter of restoring the data to what it was before they touched it. The frightening thing was that on paper they were excellent.

In those days I relied heavily on temp agencies, but it began to feel as though they were better at gathering CVs than they were at vetting candidates. It also proved to me that qualifications without experience can be hopeless.

When I started the bookkeeping part of the business, I would accept freelance jobs at client sites. I would arrive at a company and apart from a briefing about what they did I was left to get on with it and that is what I did. I assumed that any one sent to me would be capable of doing the same. I could not have been more wrong.

The first big mistake I made was giving too much work up front before I had a feel for what they could do. I did not check intermittently to see how they were getting on. I was careful not to give them work that was messy or complicated, but I must admit, I resented that, because that is a lot of what we are expected to do, clean up other people's record keeping messes.

I also was not clear about what I expected them to have completed within the time allotted and to what standard.

And to add insult to injury, I was paying a high daily rate, but I needed a resource that did not require any minimum commitment so I accepted I would pay more for that; but at the very least expected a minimum standard of work.

At the time I saw it as a total failing on the part of the agency(s), but it taught me things about my business model that were not going to work for me and forced me to address them. Ultimately the failure of the exercise came back to my own lack of planning and checking.

For one, ad hoc temps were too expensive and there was no consistency because I could not guarantee I would get the same person each time I needed someone. This posed problems for me, not just in terms of consistency of skills but also privacy and confidentiality, even though using accountancy temps is a common way of finding personnel. I knew it was not me for other than for sporadic needs, and if the business was to grow I needed to put in place resources that would support that growth.

My organisation chart and role specification needed revising dramatically.

I went back to the drawing board and asked myself what the ideal associate would look like and that is what I went looking for. It did not take long because I was so particular. It really narrowed the pool that I could choose from.

In the meantime, I had also started documenting my business processes, specifically the internal processes that dealt with what happened once a prospect turned into a customer. This included book-keeping instructions for each customer based on a standard template.

After negotiations and acceptance of terms and conditions, I started to give tasks to my new work-force. Even though, as with my previous temps my new resource was more than qualified on paper, I gave them relatively small and straightforward tasks to do that would not be too disastrous if they did not carry them out accurately.

For example, one of them only ever entered sales invoices on the accounts systems and then either I or Gill would double check them when we reconciled the customers' bank accounts and carried out month-end checks. They did such a good job that I added purchases to their remit and similarly checked them in the same way. Everybody received a copy of the customers book-keeping instructions which covered any items specific to that client and this reduced the number of queries that they had. In fact when there were queries my usual response was "agree with your treatment - that's correct" or it required us to go back to the client for missing information as opposed to it being a lack of knowledge.

I cannot even begin to describe how liberating this was.

The other lesson I learned was that it is important to organise the given information and this enables the provider to do a better job. In my case, I was sorting out a core part of the business, in most of your cases it will be non-core tasks so the amount of detail that I went into will not be necessary. There should be check points to follow or; at least do so in the early stages. We at Precision Services and Financial Gym instigate check points so we know if we are meeting the client's needs.

A reputable outsource provider will have built in reporting mechanisms and ways to keep you informed, but if not, make it your business to ensure you are updated. This may take the form of progress updates, as in the case of web design. Results and return on investment as in the case of PR and marketing assistance (even if you are already measuring this yourself). Regular Financial Management reports from your bookkeeper or accountant. What increase in connections on Twitter have you had over a period of time if using a provider to handle your social media activity?

As your relationship develops; and depending on the service this will become less necessary as a monitoring mechanism and more as a way to keep you updated.

Despite the improvement in my handling of using additional resources, please do not let me mislead you into believing there were no hitches at all. Situations will always arise that you did not anticipate, but if the basic are in place they will be exceptions only and the good thing about challenges (we will not call them problems) is that they force you to up your game. All new relationships need time for the parties to adjust to each other. Hiccups are commonly not down to fault but a symptom of the relationship being in the early stages. Good planning will minimise this.

Outsourcing is Not Abdicating

The goal is to let go of the doing, maintain control but without being a bottleneck in the process.

The point I made in the Baby Steps section about having check points and being kept informed cannot be stressed enough. Now while I know from personal experience that the relief of having repetitive and time consuming tasks taken away is liberating in itself, do not make the mistake of totally abdicating all responsibility for the success of the required outcome. This is still your business after all; and yes, while the goal is to finally escape from the drudgery of trying to do everything, still be mindful of whatever is being done, it is being done in your name. It is great to have someone else manage and post your blogs for example, but be alert to whether the blogs truly do reflect you and your business and the message you want to put out there.

I remember a few years ago meeting a client of mine who is an electrical contractor at one of the sites he was working on to get some paperwork signed. When I got there he was fuming because one of his electrical sub-contractors had finished a job, but had left the place in a mess and there was a little exposed wiring. Nothing dangerous but below the standard he prided himself on. He then began to wonder how many other jobs had been concluded like this. Why this came down to him I will cover later, but it may be that this was a fluke and the other jobs were fine, but the fact is he did not know. In fairness to the sub-contractor, his brief was to go out and fix electrical problems and that is what he did. To the owner of the company he prided himself on not only providing electrical repairs and rewiring but on the overall impression that his customers were left with.

With my packages, one of the key selling points has always been regular management reporting. However despite being one of the reasons an entrepreneur decided to work with me; they did not look at them as a matter of habit. It was only when things were not going right; that emails would arrive asking for the very information they have been getting to date. If they had been looking at them they would possibly have seen a pattern emerging.

The way I deal with this now is to instigate regular contact; either with my company or their accountant.

Even those who are converts to the idea of having an external provider may actually see the letting go in itself as the end result; and completely ignore or neglect the added benefits, in my case steady financial data.

Also you may still be required to contribute at some level, usually in time and resource but at a much reduced level than if you were doing it all yourself. Even though you may not be doing the book-keeping and accounts anymore, someone at your end still has to collate the information to hand over, which takes much less time than doing it yourself. But if you want to get a book-keeper or accountant on their soapbox, get them going on the subject of getting paperwork out of clients and watch the frustration take over.

A very good letting agent client of mine started out working on his own with one part-time lady and he personally used to sort out the paperwork for me. To say it took time would be an understatement, but to his credit he is a true entrepreneur and from day one farmed out the book-keeping even though he could barely afford it.

The handing over of paperwork was just not of interest to him as he only wanted to sell. We knew however that this was only a temporary state of affairs because with the momentum in his company firmly behind making sales and getting landlords, we knew in time he would be able to hand that to someone else. He now has 11 members of staff who all have customer facing roles except for one, all other functions are still outsourced and he has long moved away from document handling. Every month, on the nose, he expects to have his profit and loss report arrive in his inbox.

Not to sound too corny, I am very proud of him and that business and even though times and money were tough to begin with, he never wavered from his original plan of being a business owner and not a business grafter.

CHAPTER 7

Financial Fitness - The Pulse of Business Heal

Essential Information for Financial Fitness

There are a number of differences that separate successful entrepreneurs from those that get stuck in financial survival or end up in financial crisis.

1. Successful business owners know accurately where they are financially and they know where they are going

2. They have a clear idea of the problems they face and they have plans to deal with them

3. They generally take action before problems occur because they have the information to anticipate them

Let's look at some of the mechanisms they use to do this that would apply to even the smallest of business owner.

Business Financial Planning – No Matter How Small You Are

Although this book is intended for those of you who have been in business for a while, it can be very useful to act like a start-up. Some of you may be starting over as a completely new entity, possibly after a previous business collapse; you will be going back to the drawing board and totally overhauling your business. Or this may be genuinely your first foray into entrepreneurship after a successful career in employment.

With this in mind I will start at the beginning.

Now I know it seems like work but as I stated before in Chapter Five – Planning Your Freedom, having a working business plan is a fundamental component of robust financial figures. Whether your plan is a 30 page document or a one page mind map, it will form the benchmark for your progress. In this chapter, I will only touch on the financial components that your require. Please do accept that no aspect of your plan can be considered in isolation. The different areas, whether it be sales and marketing; product mix; personnel and resources and of course the finances. All impact on each other.

The financial section of a business plan should include:

- Start-up costs analysis – applicable

- Sales forecast

- Break-even analysis

- Budget/profit and loss forecast

- Balance sheet forecast

- Cashflow forecast

Now before you have a coronary, it does not have to be you that produces these. If you can do them yourself that is great; as I believe it is a great way to really get to grips with the numbers but there are other options. Requesting an accountant or book-keeper to set them up for you is a good idea and then you can maintain them, or they can do both. Whatever method you choose, for the purpose of starting a fresh or revamping your business; your input is imperative because you are going to be in the driver's seat and responsible for turning the forecasts into a reality.

Financial forecasts with little or no history to refer to are by their very nature incorrect. They are often based on guesswork, assumptions and more than a large pinch of enthusiasm or pessimism in some cases. That is why monitoring the actual results against your forecasts once you start trading is crucial so you can see how far off the mark you were; understand why this is; and either revise your forecasts accordingly or take steps to achieve them. Unless the forecasts were drastically unrealistic the target is to do the latter.

Start-up Costs Analysis

Some businesses can require quite a lot of money to get off the ground, particularly if they are going to trade from rented premises, need equipment, vehicles and possibly staff from the beginning. Others can get away with an office from home and very little initial outlay. The point is to know what is needed and establish how it will be paid for.

It is also advisable to build a cushion of money into the equation as sales can be lower than expected for longer than expected and that is not taking into account credit that may have to be given to customers. Add to the mix expenses possibly being more than expected and some suppliers could require cash on delivery. The business could be under immense cash pressure disaster before it has had a chance to establish itself properly.

Sales Forecast

Sales forecasting is how many sales you plan to make over a given period to not only cover your expenses but to create the profit the business will need if to progress as planned. At least a 12 month forecast is advisable, particularly if the business is seasonal, so any peaks and troughs can be accounted for to ensure your expenses can be covered throughout the year.

Sales Break-even figure

This is the level of sales you need to make to ensure you start making enough money to cover your expenses. Below this level, the business is running at a loss and running out of money is a consequence.

See the example below:

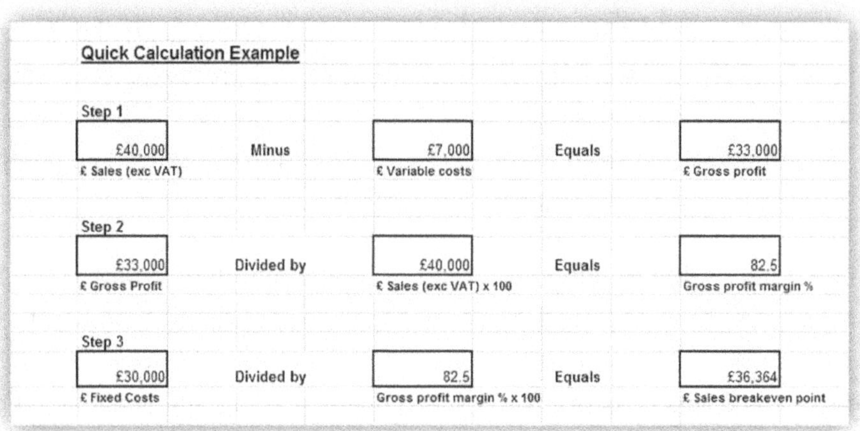

Enter numbers in green boxes only

To obtain a working Excel copy of this template send an email to: info@financialgymforbusiness.com

Budget/Profit & Loss Forecast/Statement

A record of how much money a business is making over a given period of time.

Balance Sheet

A statement of what a business is worth at any given time

Cash Flow Forecast/Statement

Tracks when money actually comes in and goes out of the company, as opposed to a profit and loss which is based on the period sales and expenses due.

Few businesses utilise all reports all of the time, though it would be advantageous if they did. Start-up costs are obviously only at the beginning. However for example you may establish what your break-even figure is, but not revise again unless your overheads change.

CHAPTER 8

Financial Fitness Results – Making Sense of Financial Reports

I am not going to go into too great a depth on this topic as to most entrepreneurs like yourself; the thought of wading through lots of information about financial statements is probably your idea of hell. So I am going attempt to keep it as basic as possible.

For those of you who really want an in-depth guide to understanding your financial records, there are lots of sources of information such as the Internet, your book-keeper; your accountant and of course, Financial Gym. Also note that I use the terms financial reports and management reports interchangeably.

Below is my illustration of the relationship between the main types of financial/management reports.

This diagram shows the activity cycle based on a month, but you can substitute month for week, quarter or year.

Budget

(Profit and Loss Forecast)

How much profit do I plan to make over a period of time whether it is a month, a week, a year, etc?

What level of sales am I forecasting?

What will it cost me to make those sales?

What other expenses (overheads) will I incur each period to enable to me to run my business as a whole?

I prefer to call this report a profit and loss forecast because the word budget is so entrenched in personal finances and is generally a tool to train you to stay within your financial means, and to not spend more than you earn.

Whereas if you are planning for a successful growing business; you want to be budgeting for an increase in income and profit. This way you are always looking at a moving target, in the upwards trajectory. Just like trying to build and tone muscles as part of a fitness regime, the muscles become used to being worked at a particular weight and stop responding, therefore it is necessary to keep increasing the weight or resistance to achieve the overall target.

info@financialgymforbusiness.com

Balance Sheet

The balance sheet is the focal report for determining the ability of the business to grow and is worth something to you as well as to outsiders. It addresses questions such as:

- What is my business worth at this date?

- How much do I own?

- How much is owed to me compared to how much I owe to others?

- Is my business solid enough to carry me through to the next period?

- Is my business a good prospect for borrowing, investment or for sale?

Anatomy of a Balance Sheet

Profit and Loss

How much profit did I make over a period of time, whether it is a month, a week, a year, etc?

What is my level of sales?

What does it cost me to make those sales?

What other expenses do I incur each period to enable to me to run the business as a whole?

Anatomy of a Profit and Loss Statement

Profit & Loss Report Breakdown

Sales:
Products I sold this month

Services I sold this month
Add

Opening Stock:
Items I can sell I had at the beginning of the month
Add

Purchases:
Items I bought during the month to sell
Minus

Closing Stock: Items I have left over ready to sell next month
Equals

Gross Profit/Loss:
Minus

Direct Costs:
e.g. Packaging, delivery, subcontractors
Equals

Operating Profit/Loss:
Money to pay business expenses
Minus

Fixed Costs:
Wages, Rent, Utilities, Telephone, Insurance, Fuel, etc
Equals

Net Profit/Loss:
Money left to pay yourself e.g. dividends, bonus, investments, (after taxes)

Cash Flow Analysis

This predicts the actual money coming in and going out of your business over a given period of time. This can be weekly, monthly or quarterly. When money is tight it is a good idea to have a daily analysis. Really efficient business owners track the actual cash flow compared to the forecast to see if the predicted amounts of money are really materialising.

Even profitable companies fail if they do not have adequate money to cover their expenses as and when needed. Bills are paid with cash – not profit.

Anatomy of a Cash Flow Forecast

Cashflow Forecast Breakdown

Cash In :
Loans Received

Cash received from customers

Minus

Cash Out:
Expenses: as on Profit and Loss

Loan repayments

Taxes paid out

Add

Cash left at the End of the month:

Add

Cash in the bank from previous month:
Or overdraft amount, if that is the case

Equals

Cash Available to fund next month's expenses:

CHAPTER 9

Raising Finance & Borrowing

With the economic conditions as they have been since 2007/2008, I know this could be the topic that represents the straw that broke the camel's back. I have personally witnessed the stress and anxiety of some of my clients caused by a dwindling of their access to additional finance just when they need it the most.

The impact of this has had a number of effects; one being, businesses that relied on borrowing and credit have battened down the hatches and cut back expenditure dramatically They have also, actually gone out of business because their use of credit was disguising the fact that the business was actually insolvent or not even commercially viable. With the criteria for lending being more stringent than it has been for years, even for those businesses that have good track records, it is no wonder that so many business people have gone into hibernation waiting for the winter to pass.

I am personally biased towards not owing anybody anything but depending on the type of business and the future plans, there may well come a point when in order to move your business to the next level; additional funding will be an essential factor in making that happen. Without the extra injection of cash, some plans just cannot be realised, particularly if you do not have enough cash/assets of your own.

I will touch on some of the things to think about before going down the borrowing route and if you still believe it is for you, the next part will give a better understanding about the bank criteria for lending.

Considerations before Seeking Finance

1. Start up finance only needed

2. Will the money be used to cover day-to-day operating expenses? – Consider why your trading activities are not covering your expenses and address that first. Borrowing will just exacerbate an already precarious situation. Conventional lending institutions are unlikely to lend to you under those circumstances anyway.

3. To clear debts – borrowing to cover borrowing is on a par with needing money to cover day to day expenses. You could make the situation worse or totally unmanageable. If it is due to temporary circumstances (how long has it been temporary?) and the extending of your overdraft for a few months will get you over a hump; then it may well be a risk worth taking.

4. You are buying fixed assets (also called capital expenditure) such as new equipment or property. Whether to increasing assets/investments in the case of property or increasing the scale and capacity of its operations in the case of equipment. This would be viewed as a more feasible reason by lending institutions.

5. You are funding growth – the best motive for enquiring into types of borrowing and one of the reasons most likely to be of interest to outside investors. There is a projected return on their investment which means you can repay your lender or investor while increasing the profitability of the business.

6. Do you need the money for other short-term or long-term reasons?

7. Do you need a lump sum or regular periodic injections of cash?

8. What is your ability to repay any borrowings or investment?

Types of Borrowing or Funding

This is merely a list of some of the options available to most self employed and small business owners. I make no judgment on the choice of any over the other. This is a matter based on individual circumstances and should be assessed on each particular situation. Also some are more easily obtainable than others, and not all financing options are available to all types of business. At one time remortgaging was a fairly easy way to realise cash, but with the dawn of the credit crunch it seemed mortgage deals dried up overnight.

- Personal savings

- Personal loan

- Personal credit cards

- Family and friends

- Remortgaging

- Business loan

- Business grants

- Community development finance institutions

- Peer-to-peer lending

- Asset finance (leasing, contract hire)

- Invoice finance/factoring

- Crowdfunding

- Bartering

- Bootstrapping

Angel and Venture Capital Investment

This is in reality not an option for the majority of small businesses. There is rarely enough equity/profit to be of interest to an investor. In other words the company is not worth enough to be able to afford to not only repay any original investment but also to provide the investor with a healthy return on their investment.

Small businesses can and do attract angel investors because as individuals they are more flexible about who and what they invest in. However the number of angel investors who lose money on failed businesses is quite high, so the terms may be quite stringent and as such out of the reach of the average small business. For the self-employed it is not really even a consideration.

What Are Lenders Looking For?

I am going to use borrowing from banks as the basis for this section because it is the lending institution that is common to all businesses whether you choose them or not and the principles of dealing with them translates to most other types of institutional lender.

Whether in business or not, there can be few adults who are not aware that the banks have become more risk sensitive than probably ever before. At least in my lifetime, I remember being able to call my bank on the phone asking for an increase in my overdraft, getting a yes there and then and then being able to draw on it within days.

Then as time went on it became a little more difficult and it became more likely to be asked for guarantees of some description depending on type and amount of borrowing required. This signing of a personal guarantee from you or a third party promises to honour the payment of the loan in case the business should fail. Another way is taking a charge against your business often in the form of a debenture. This means that the company signs over specific assets to the lender as security. For example the client base, property (if the business owns any), capital equipment, in fact any asset that if sold could provide the money to repay the loan. This stops the business from being able to sell the assets because that option now belongs to the lender/issuer of the debenture. This way if the business fails to pay and ends up in default, the lender can get their money back.

Before approaching a bank I cannot emphasize enough how important it is to be able to view borrowing from their viewpoint. Ignore this and kiss goodbye to a yes.

Top of the list – you need a well put together business plan.

Ignore the movies, the days of putting on your best suit and going to see the stern bank manager who softens when they realise how passionate you are and lends you the money because you "know this can work" are firmly in the realms of urban myth. No plan, no money.

If you do not have the skills to do one, get a professional to do it for you. Bear in mind the business plan you have for your own business may need to be tweaked or even changed dramatically. Your current one may be more of a working document geared towards what you need to do to build the business and may be very internal in its language. When preparing one for a lender the emphasis needs to be geared toward how viable your business is and its ability to "comfortably" pay back any borrowing. The information will be the same but how you present it must cater to what the lender needs to see. Make it easier for them to say yes to you. Your current business plan is usually about what is in it for you and your target market.

This one will be about what is in it for the banks.

There are no guarantees but anything you can do to influence the outcome in your favour is worth the effort. A lack of, or poorly prepared business plan will set you up for disappointment.

Campari Is More than Just a Drink

Banks have different methods of assessing loan applications and these vary from bank to bank and from time to time. And even if the assessment process stays the same, the criteria for passing the process can change. Think how credit scoring differs from bank to bank, meaning you are turned down for a credit card by one bank, but get it with ease from another.

The method that I am familiar with is called CAMPARI. It is by no means the only one, but it is a good paradigm to work from.

CAMPARI stands for:

- Character
- Ability
- Margin
- Purpose
- Amount
- Repayment
- Insurance

Character

This part is interested in how trustworthy you are personally:

- How dedicated to the business are you?
- Does your age and health support your plans?
- What is your past history with credit?
- Do you have any personal assets?
- Ability

- This relates to how equipped you, your team and the business is to carry out the plans proposed for the business. Do you even have a team or is everything based on you?

- What would happen if you were unable to carry on in the business for any reason?

- What is your business history?

- Do you have previous business successes and failures?

- What is your or your team's experience of the field of business you are in or is this a change of direction?

- Do you understand financial reports and can demonstrate how they will be achieved?

- Have you been successfully controlling the business to date or has it been constant fire fighting?

Margin

Let us not forget, banks are in business to make money and they need to compare how much money they can make out of you to how risky a prospect you are.

How much commission, fees, interest etc will they be able to earn from lending to you?

Purpose

This is the reason you need the money.

Not everything is eligible for lending. Banks may deem some sectors more risky than others for e.g. restaurants and leisure industry businesses were shied away from by at least one bank I know, they didn't even bother to get the application in. Or the bank may think it is actually illegal to trade in the way proposed by the borrower.

Is the money to finance planned strategy or to solve a problem or emergency? (See "Considerations before Seeking Finance" above)

Will the money realistically achieve this purpose? Is the entrepreneur being naive?

Does the bank agree with you? Business owners who need money have been known to ask for one purpose while it is really for something else. They say expansion but it is really to keep the VAT man at bay.

What evidence do you have to back up your reasons? Think of entrepreneurs on Dragons Den when they say they have big orders in the pipeline and that is why they need the money. The Dragons invariably ask them to verify this with a letter of intent from the buyer or an actual order placed.

Do they agree with you on this idea? You may be planning for expansion and the bank thinks you should merely consolidate at this stage.

Amount

How much money do you want to borrow?

Based on your business plan forecasts and performance to date is the amount realistic, or are you asking for too much or too little? Too much and you may struggle to meet the payments, too little and you will run out of cash too soon and need to borrow again.

Do your cash flow forecasts lead the lender to a different amount?

Repayment

This is the crux of the assessment, how is the loan to be repaid and over what length of time?

The usual measure in a business is based on the profits made that turn into available cash, but there are others such as the sale of an asset that will yield enough money to cover the loan with interest.

Established businesses are at an advantage here as they have historical trading figures to work from whereas start-ups do not and must provide another way to prove their financial standing.

Is this the first loan for the business? If you have had one previously and repaid it successfully then this will work in your favour.

Insurance

In the unfortunate event your business was unable to meet the loan payments what could you offer to the bank as security that they could use to repay the loan? Preferably something they could easily value and sell. Banks will inform you what security or collateral are within their lending criteria.

Over to You

Work through the CAMPARI criteria and answer the questions based on your own personal circumstances. Even if you are not planning to borrow in the near future; the answers will give you a personal insight into your financial standing that you may have been unaware of until now. By highlighting any areas of weakness you will then know what you need to strengthen in your financial foundations.

CHAPTER 10

Record Keeping to Stay Out of Trouble

Regardless of the size of your business you need to keep book-keeping records. The success of your financial planning and analysis hinges on how accurate these records are at any given time.

Common Scenarios for Disaster

- Poor book-keeping records due to lack of knowledge and experience.

- Inaccurate book-keeping records – recording items as one thing when it should be recorded as something else if proper accounts are to be produced.

- Incomplete book-keeping – e.g. not reconciling bank statements with your own records.

- Inconsistent/irregular book-keeping – nothing done for ages and then all done in one go, and that is assuming it is done up-to-date.

- Poor or sketchy knowledge of what is allowed and not allowed for tax purposes

Consequences of Not Having a Good Book-Keeping System

- They form the basis from which budget, cash flow forecasts, profit and loss information can be created. Otherwise figures are little more than guesswork.

- Year-end accounts and self assessment tax returns cannot be properly produced without correct bookkeeping

- VAT return figures are unreliable

- People with poor bookkeeping systems tend to end up paying more to their accountants because time needs to be spent doing what should have been done during the year.

- Often end up paying late penalty charges to HMRC because accounts are produced late

- Frequently unable to pay tax and VAT on time because of not having accurate up-to-date records to enable them to be planned for.

Things to Consider When Setting Up Your Book-Keeping/Accounting System

1. Paper based systems are fine when you are starting out; but for growing businesses they are not flexible enough. You end up with a record of transactions but no reports without having to create them manually.

2. Spreadsheets, typically given by accountants for your use during the year; have the same limitations of paper-based systems. Though more flexible, you still end up either manually trying to create reports or relying on your accountant to do it. Usually only at the end of the year, too late for making critical, timely management decisions.

3. If you are not confident with accounting software, there are cut-down options for start-up businesses or for those with few transactions, so you can get used to using the product and then upgrade if and when you think it is necessary.

4. If you are not confident when it comes to accounting software, seek advice. You may just need pointing in the right direction with a little training to get you on your way.

5. However, if you are not happy to do this or feel that your time in the business would be better spent in other areas i.e. income generating; then there are various options for outsourcing this side of the business, whether you are a one person operation working from home or a larger company.

6. HM Revenue and Customs as of 2011 started carrying out record checks .i.e. looking at the way businesses keep their day-to- day book-keeping records. They were particularly targeting micro and small businesses as they are deemed most likely to have incomplete records. Businesses whose records do not meet the required criteria face financial penalties

7. Even if your book-keeping is good, the best financial reports are of no use if they are not produced and reviewed regularly. This is the only way to catch problems early. You have a better chance of turning around a bad month than a bad quarter or bad year.

8. If you are an entrepreneur who is in need of sales or in the process of positioning your business for success, it is financial madness to prioritise doing book-keeping over getting money in. Generating income must always come first. Unless of course you do book-keeping for a living. Are you putting other jobs to one side to do accounts? Is this the best way to grow? How much money do you make when you do your accounts?

CHAPTER 11

Accountant Or Bookkeeper – Which Do You Need?

What an Accountant Does For You

The title accountant covers a number of different roles and jobs and what one accountant is expert in can be somewhat different to another accountant.

Also note that it is not compulsory to have particular qualifications to call yourself an accountant. Even though the majority in private practice do have them, many are "qualified by experience" (QBE). However there are certain duties that require qualification such as auditing and forensic accounting, to name a couple. They carry much higher levels of risk and responsibility by their very nature. So the implications of getting such projects wrong can result in such disastrous consequences that it would be unlikely that an unqualified or uninsured accountant would be hired in the first place.

However even qualifications and insurance is not enough in some cases, (Google the Enron and Arthur Anderson scandal of 2001, it is a fascinating story). I will keep it simple and concentrate on the functions that they perform as opposed to what type of accountant they are.

Management Accounting

The regular production of reports such as profit and loss, balance sheets, cash flows, etc; for the benefit of analysis and interpretation of your business. As discussed in the previous chapter, the accurate production of these reports is the result of book-keeping activities. Your accountant may not be best placed to provide these as often as needed because they do not have the access that your book-keeper does and a good book-keeping service should be doing this anyway.

Accountants often get around this by taking advantage of online products and facilities that require you, the business owner to enter your data online and they can then log on and see what you have been doing. However this is still not greatly appealing to the busy entrepreneur because it still requires them to do the donkey work or to assign other staff to do it, who may be better utilised elsewhere in the business.

Compliance

This includes the preparation of year end accounts, tax calculations and checking that the business activities revealed in your accounts are within the financial and legal boundaries to make sure you do not fall foul of the authorities. This will also include filing the accounts at Companies House and HMRC.

If the book-keeping data the accountant is working from is of a good standard, then the production of these reports should be a straightforward process and will only be complicated if you have complex affairs. This is obviously why accountants prefer data from book-keepers because less time is spent sorting out errors, manipulating client spreadsheets or chasing clients for missing paperwork and information.

In the early days people would ask me if using a book-keeper would reduce their accountancy fees and I would be able to say yes with some degree of confidence, for the reasons I described above.

However accountants are themselves in business and lowering fees are not in their interests. Even the smaller practices are becoming more adept at maximising their own margins than ever before; and why not? They need to eat too. My only issue is when the pricing policy of some practices does not offer good value to the client. So many business people regard getting their accountant to produce financial statements as a necessary evil. Accountancy fees can feel very much like a punitive cost. Particularly if they do not read, understand or use the information the accountant provides.

Imagine if at the end of the year, or even better, every few months, instead of the bulk of your fees being swallowed up by the time taken to get your financial statements together, the time was used to discuss your business performance overall and to look at its long term future. I hear the complaints of my contacts and clients about the lack of support some of them feel they get from their accountants, and I do not dispute that there are the ones that feel the world ends at compliance and as long as they are good at that, job done.

But I firmly believe that the majority welcomes the opportunity to give a more comprehensive service that reflects the expertise and experience they have; and often it is the low value placed on this by clients that make it difficult.

Strategy and Planning

How often have you been given your accounts and/or tax bill by your accountant and found that your tax bill is higher than expected or some area of your accounts for the previous year is working against you? You find yourself thinking "why are you telling me now when it is too late to do anything about it."

If you have the compliance minded accountant, then this a big part of the problem, but if you do not and you have an accountant who really wants to work with your business, then it may be worth taking a long, hard look at your contribution to the relationship and see whether the bottleneck of information may well lie with you.

If this is the case, by not dealing with it you will miss out on the opportunity to truly get your money's worth from your accountant, and that is by enabling them to provide you with help in the actual strategy and planning of your business goals. Not just when it comes to tax planning, but with regards to growth and planning for success. Much of the skills that we hire management or business consultants for can be more than handled by a proactive accountant. If deep in your soul you are more concerned with not paying tax than you are with growing a sustainable, successful business, then this is a conversation that you will not instigate.

If however you are truly committed to achieving the financial success you really desire, before you start spending money you probably do not have yet, explore with your accountant other ways that they can start to be of real value to you.

Firstly, you and your business will seem a lot more interesting a prospect to your accountant who will see more value in you as a client – let's not pretend they are a charity. This hopefully precipitates a shift in your relationship from one of client and supplier to one of business associates. Immediately you will have added to your strategic financial team. Also one of the grievances expressed by clients is that they feel stupid when they deal with their accountant because it is implied that they know little. Even if you do know very little; the fact that you are approaching them with an attitude of getting results will see you go right up in your accountant's estimations. I know you are not trying to win a popularity contest, but the fact is when we respect someone and what they stand for we treat them very differently. Become that valued client because if you do what you plan to do financially you really will be.

I have been very lucky to have been able to work with some wonderful accountants and they have been so grateful to find that their client has invested in added a book-keeping service to their financial team because not only can they produce the compliance work more quickly but they can now get on and do what they do best. The questions that they used to ask of the business owner, they would direct to me, because they would get a quicker response and in the format they required it.

What a Bookkeeper Does for You

To whom this may concern: accountants make poor book-keepers. Not because they can't do it, though many can't, but for a number of reasons some of which are:

- They have spent so many years removed from it that it is no longer easy for them to do.

- They are more proficient with accounts production software than book-keeping software.

- Some have never really done it in earnest from day one.

- Others do it as a way of having a reason to keep the client close and often sub-contract it back to someone like me, so the client is paying accountancy rates for book-keeping and it is being done by someone they could have hired directly.

Have you ever had a procedure booked via private healthcare, gone to the hospital to find it is the same doctor you would have had on the NHS? The same scenario, but without the obvious advantages.

Accountants are not book-keepers with extras, they are accountants. The Institute of Certified Bookkeepers (ICB) is the largest professional dedicated book-keeping body in the world. Known for having stringent marking, less than around 80% is a fail on many exams. At the time of writing this, they have a fast-track examination especially designed for accounting and book-keeping professionals who qualify for exemption from going through the full examination process, whether due to qualification or experience.

Head of ICB Gary Carter once admitted that at one time the percentage of accountants that failed the exam was over 90%. It may well still be the case. Book-keeping and accounting are different disciplines with different emphasis.

A book-keeping service will:

- Systemise your accounting processes

- Keep track of your daily accounting records and run payroll

- Provide records to allow filing of periodic returns such as VAT and PAYE.

- Produce monthly, quarterly, annual management reports

- Cash flow forecasts and budgets

- Some will do the final accounts.

- Be the shoulder to cry on and a sounding board day-to-day.

CHAPTER 12

Failing Health -
Alarm Bells of Financial Trouble

Business failure is a very easy concept to grasp. It simply means you have run out of cash. All the action in a business is to achieve one main tangible aim. Produce a surplus of cash. Without that, all the other goals, personal or professional, have no chance of being accomplished.

Stages of Failure
Downturn - Some Early Failure Signs

- Sales have stayed constant for a long period of time or are declining

- Profit and loss shows profit has been stagnating for months. There may even be periodic losses that are not due to legitimate reasons. E.g. a seasonal business that makes most of its money at certain times of the year and just ticks over for the rest would not be alarmed by occasional losses because it would be balanced out over the year. But other businesses need to keep profit up continuously so this would constitute cause for concern.

- First signs of returned direct debits, standing orders and cheques you issue bouncing

- Payments that took you slightly over your overdraft that were previously let through by your bank stop being honoured by them. The bank is taking precautions, due to the slightly more uncertain banking activity in your account.

- You take longer to pay supplier bills

Decline - Getting Worse

- Need to apply for or to increase the overdraft to compensate for sustained downturn in profit

- Hire small equipment which you previously would have purchased outright

- Experience intermittent difficulty in getting credit.

- Occasional chasing letter

- Consider business coaching with a view to reversing poor performance, rather than as a way of growing business

- Take the option of Invoice Finance/Factoring a little more seriously

Disintegration – Writing on the wall

- Direct debits, standing orders and cheques being returned or bouncing has become a regular occurrence

- Account is overdrawn or in overdraft as often if not more often than it is in the black

- Pay suppliers and overheads in dribs and drabs (payments on account) rather in full as a desperate attempt to hang on to money longer

- Pay bills with personal money with a view to paying yourself back, but not able to take the money back out due to lack of funds

- Suppliers put you on stop or only take orders if you pay at the time by cash or credit card

- Late or missed VAT and PAYE payments to the Revenue and hit with late payment fines and penalties

- Receive regular chasing letters, some now threaten legal action.

- You pay the suppliers that are most likely to take action rather than because their bills are due

- Bailiffs visit your premises to recover outstanding monies

- Get unsolicited sales letters from debt management companies offering help

- You avoid taking calls unless you know who it is

Reasons for Business Failure

The reasons for business failure are as numerous as they are varied but whatever the specifics of any particular situation they usually come under 3 areas:

- Inadequate Financial Performance and Controls

- Inadequate Operational Performance and Controls

- Inadequate Business Owner Performance and Controls

Inadequate Financial performance and controls include:

- Not enough sales or customers on a consistent basis to cover costs and to make a profit

- Not enough profit or sustained losses

- Poor credit control – invoices not sent out promptly and outstanding money not collected from customers quickly enough with unclear or un-enforced terms and conditions

- Constant negative cash flow often caused by selling goods on credit terms that you have had to pay for up front – particularly if credit situation is poor with suppliers

- Too much stock lying around that is not selling or being used to generate sales fast enough which is tying up money you need to use for more immediate expenses

- Money tied up in large assets such as machinery and vehicles that are also not generating income or under-utilised. Do you have assets that should be in use 5 days a week but stand idle for 2 or more?

- Growing too quickly or taking on large jobs without ensuring there is ample money to fund the growth or project.

- Regularly rectifying customer complaints by compensating them financially, e.g. credits, refunds, returns and freebies, rather than improving service levels

- Poor financial accounting systems and reporting, inadequate book-keeping

- Not understanding or able to interpret financial reports and no clear idea how to use the information from the financial reports to improve business.

Inadequate Operational Performance and controls include:

Only one person in charge. To emphasise the point again and as difficult as this is to swallow, businesses with only one person at the helm are more likely to fail because of the lack of support and because it is limited to the knowledge, experience and energy of one person.

The Danger of the Number One

This principle, although not mine I might add, is well-known and one of the main motivators behind my decision to go against the traditional book-keeping model.

One of anything in a business can be trouble. Only one way of earning income, only one person who knows how to perform a task, only one bank account, only one product or service that is available to sell, only one way to collect money, only one way of being contacted, only one method of attracting customers, etc.

The results show up in a number of ways:-

- Staff or workers with insufficient skills, training or enthusiasm for the job

- The standard of output dependent on who is doing job or task so lacks consistency.

- People in business who are expert in their field or industry but not in running a business or giving good customer service.

- Systems and procedures (if any) set for benefit of business owner rather than to enhance customer experience

- Lack of suitable equipment to get the job done, 'making do' equipment.

- No way of measuring performance internally and externally (e.g. customer feedback)

Business Owner

There are a multitude of examples here; do you recognise any of them in yourself or a fellow business owner?

- Runs around doing lots of things but has no real strategy so nothing really solved long-term

- Aware of problems, has a plan of action but does not follow through at all, or consistently enough for results to show.

- Sees warning signs as normal. There is a credit crunch after all and it is happening to other similar businesses. Equate situation to external forces such as the state of the economy and do not take into account their own performance.

- Completely unaware that the problem is growing. Possibly due to being misled by inaccurate management reports as a result of poor book-keeping.

- Cash in the bank is the main gauge for cash flow performance so sudden downturn in available cash is a surprise.

- Relies on annual accounts with no data in between

- So afraid of making things worse and not sure where to turn to for help so carry on as they are indefinitely in the hope things will get better

CHAPTER 13

Turning Things Around

Know Your Exact Position

Get Your Books Up-to-Date!!

You have to be able to produce the information you need to enable you to understand your true financial position, otherwise how can you come up with an effective plan of action? Without these, nobody will be able to offer you advice and support of any real value as they will have nothing tangible to use as a benchmark to work with.

Like most things worth doing or having, there is a cost attached, and investing in financial support is one of them. Rest assured once systems and processes are up and running you should be able to see the benefits in a matter of weeks. Even if this is just in the reduction of time and resources previously used for book-keeping being directed elsewhere, coupled with the availability of the information you really need.

Re-Evaluate Your Targets and Projections – Future Plans

It is imperative that you know whether your actual performance is slipping compared to your forecasted performance. If they are, is it because you are underperforming or were your original projections unrealistic to begin with?

A favourite question that entrepreneurs are asked or ask of themselves is how much more money they plan to make in future years compared to the current one. Whether the question is asked is relation to sales or profit, it is astonishing how often the answer is "double" year on year. A clear indication that they do not really know at all or they are driven by enthusiasm rather than facts.

Take a business that has been increasing its turnover each year at a steady rate of say 20%; it would be an amazing feat for them to suddenly see their sales increase by 100% without any major changes taking place, particularly in tough times. If this has been the basis of measuring achievement, then of course the results will look bad.

Now let us turn our attention back to the business that has realistic forecasts but these are not being met and the symptoms of cash flow problems as discussed in Chapter Twelve have become part of their daily existence the focus must now turn to what must be done to reverse the regression.

Just like putting on weight, the results of being financially unfit can happen slowly and go almost unnoticed; creeping up on you until one day you realise nothing fits you anymore or why you can no longer run for the bus without it taking you twice as long to get your breath back. When you decide to lose the weight or to improve your physical fitness the reversal can be equally as slow, but this time you are in control of the progression and you will be heading in the right direction. This slow deterioration can also occur in business if your financial controls, bookkeeping and reporting are weak and similarly, it may take a while before any positive changes are reflected in the reversal of your fortunes. The trick is to follow through and persevere.

The good news is there are some immediate ways of heading back onto the right track which you can implement yourself assuming the situation has not become so bad that your only option is to seek outside help or of being rescued.

Ways to Improve Your Profitability-Yourself

Do not lose sight of the most important objective, increasing or creating enough profit to generate the steady availability of cash needed to run your business.

No Profit $\rightarrow$ **No Cash** $\rightarrow$ **No Business**

Raise your prices. As an exercise, add 1% to your prices and calculate how much more you would have earned in sales in the past year with just a 1% increase. Now look at a realistic percentage increase and in one fell swoop you can improve your margins.

1. Analyse the percentage of your overall sales that each customer contributes, and ensure that no-one or few customers account for a high percentage or the majority of your sales. Many businesses rely heavily on one or a few key customers. Endeavour to avoid such a situation and so spread your risk. Envisage the devastating effect on sales and cash flow to suppliers who made the majority of their money from selling to Woolworths for example.

2. Do not give credit automatically to customers; if they request it consider credit checking. Asking for cash on delivery or in advance can minimise risk as well as speed up cash coming in. Many moons ago, I used to deal with the Cowies which became the Arriva Group who had a rule of not allowing a new customer credit until they had done business with them for at least a year, and even then you had to apply and undergo their credit checking process, as approval was still not automatic. A very large national organisation that most of us would trip over our feet to accept was refused an account because of a blip on credit reports that did not meet their credit criteria.

3. If you are aware that a new customer is switching their business from another provider to you, it would be prudent, where feasible, to know why. Particular if they are in a hurry to do business or their first order is larger than you would expect.

4. For all you know this potential customer could be experiencing cash flow problems of their own which may have resulted in the deterioration of the relationship with their previous supplier. They may even have been put on stop and are in need of a quick alternative and your business has been chosen. Again this is another reason to consider credit checking.

   As an aside; even though it is normal to request trade references as part of the checking process. Do not set too much store by them as nobody would give the name of someone who might give a bad reference and the relationship may be on friendly terms which could influence the response.

   When I first decided to venture out into the business world on my own, I could always call on a few contacts at some very high profile government offices to provide glowing references for me which I knew would impress the recipient. In fairness my contacts could hand on heart vouch that they had received good service from me in my professional dealings with them, but the reality was they were doing it as a personal favour to me.

5. Sell more. Simple enough concept to grasp but can be the hardest to achieve. If selling really is not your strength then you need to enlist the services of a person or organisation that can help you in this area. No matter what industry you are in, marketing and sales is vital, you cannot afford to do it half-heartedly simply because it is not within your comfort zone.

6. Instead of only concentrating on adding new clients, explore ways of increasing the amount you can sell to your existing customer base. This could be achieved by getting them to buy more of the same but in greater quantities. More of the same but more frequently or additional products and services. For instance a dry

cleaning business adding alterations to their list of services, or a cleaning company selling ironing to existing cleaning customers. I did this exercise a while back where I analysed how many of my book-keeping clients did not have payroll facilities

7. Offer early settlement discounts to encourage prompt payment from customers, but proceed with caution taking care to make sure discounting will not significantly eat into your profit margins.

8. Deal with customer complaints and issues promptly and satisfactorily, you cannot afford to lose good customers

9. If complaints are high or have increased. Pin down any underlying inefficiencies in your operations that are causing or contributing to this and eliminate them.

10. Fire customers - frighten away the bad payers, low profit and price sensitive customers who only want you because they believe you are cheap. Use the additional resources to add more profitable customers and enhance the service you give to the rest of your existing client base

11. If customers owe you money, collect it from them. A customer is only a customer once they have paid you, until then they are a contact or prospect or worse still, a bad debt.

12. Drop non-profitable products and services that you struggle to provide with ease or excellence. By reducing your offering in the short-term to those that can make you consistent profit, it will allow you to consolidate, improve and then expand again but this time when you are on a better financial footing and better resourced.

13. Shop around for better deals, not just for materials you use for sales but look at your overheads also. When moving suppliers be careful that you do not fall foul of any penalty charges for closing your account, particularly in the case of utility providers. Though you may find the potential savings outweigh any penalties.

14. Negotiate better terms from existing suppliers where possible. Bulk discounts, longer credit periods, etc

A word of warning before making payment agreements with creditors and government agencies – ensure you can stick to it.

I have seen too many business owners agree to payment arrangements they could not afford to stick to just to get a supplier or other creditor off their back for a while. Then before long, they find it difficult to keep to the payments leading to a situation much worse than before. This time the creditor may well have lost patience and go straight to legal or recovery action. The business owner is then faced with not only paying the full amount of what they owe in a short space of time but any additional legal and recovery costs on top. Many forced closures have been the result of a creditor, usually the tax man, losing patience because a repayment agreement has not been honoured.

15. Not one of my favourite suggestions, but sell assets to free-up cash.

Take care not to get rid of things you will need long term. E.g. do not sell the company van if you know you are going to need it again when things pick up, particularly if you will struggle to find funds to replace it. Also do not sell an asset that can still make you money. If machinery or equipment is not being utilised to their fullest, review your methods and processes that involve such machinery and equipment and see where you can be tighter. One of two things will happen, you will get your money's worth from the equipment again because you are using them more efficiently; or it will be confirmation that they are a drain on resources or no longer generating profit. In which case, they can be sold without impact on your business and generate some much needed cash.

16. If you have staff, have another look at what tasks they actually perform in the business and how good they are at them, or not as the case may be. Can anyone take on additional tasks or duties? Particularly things that you currently do yourself that you can

pass to them. You need all the time you can get to concentrate on the state of your overall business.

17. If you come to the conclusion that you have a surplus of staff for whatever reason and you have to get rid of anyone or cut their hours; run it by a human resources/employment expert. Having to deal with a claim for unfair dismissal when you are already under the cosh is a headache you can do without.

18. If you do have funds set aside and you can refrain from touching it, check it is in the best place. The amount of businesses that have funds sitting in crappy deposit accounts earning them no money simply because it is with the same bank that runs their business account and was easy to open; rather than in an account that would pay them the best return on their money.

It is not lost on me that in a tough economic climate this is hard to achieve, but the principle is the key, any extra monies you can earn even if it is just a better interest rate, why not earn it?

19. Get a mentor. One of the most important things you can do is to enlist the help of outside experts. I have talked at length about the value of looking outside to resource your business, but you also need someone to resource you. This entrepreneurial lark can be very tiring, stressful and full of the unknown. For some, a mentor is someone who impacts directly on their business. For others, they prefer to be bolstered on a more emotional level. Whatever works for you to keep you motivated then that is what you do.

I have been to more seminars and workshops than I care to count and after a few years, realised that I was becoming tired of them. A common observation about business owners is they attend events, get motivated, leave with good intentions and very little happens as the day-to-day re-sponsibilities get in the way of creativity and development. In my case it was not that, I was tired of theory and motivational speakers telling you what you should do and then sending us off with no real methods or techniques for making what they say a reality.

When I discovered Daniel Priestley and the Key Person of Influence programme, it was to work with a team of people that required activity, not just confirmation that you agreed with their philosophies so they could justify taking your money. In KPI, you are expected to get things done. Daniel has a more colourful way of putting that but you get the picture. It is your business and you can't be forced to do anything you do not want to, but unless you take action what will change?

Large businesses are used to being accountable, whether it is to shareholders, staff, other members of the management team, investors, etc. The pitfall of small business, particularly the self-employed or solopreneur, is that they only answer to themselves, so they can get away with not doing whatever they choose, even if it is imperative. They can come up with as many excuses as they like because the only person to challenge them is their own inner voice, which has been trained to go along with their decisions, even though that inner voice actually knows better.

Apart from anything else, when you are part of a team that shares common goals and attributes or you go to an expert; life is less lonely, and even if the reality of your situation is still dire, there is a sense of light at the end of the tunnel.

One of my biggest philosophies when I started out was to be an ear to listen and it is mind blowing the conversations I end up having with clients. It is a pleasure to experience a relationship with them and to move from a transactional one to a partnership.

CHAPTER 14

Business Failure – Starting Over

"You don't drown by falling in water; you only drown if you stay there."

Zig Ziglar

Despite all best efforts, it is not always possible to save a business or to avoid severe hardship while it claws its way back to viability.

If the business is at the severe deterioration stage and the turnaround strategies in the previous chapter have not worked or you simply left it too late to implement them, then the decision has to be made as to whether to take formal steps to stem the pace of deterioration.

What strategy or route you choose will depend on whether you intend to ultimately save the business as it now exists. Will you close the business entity but save its core offering so you can continue in another entity. Or will you close it with a view to walking away completely.

Formal Options

I use the term formal to differentiate from what are termed informal arrangements. Informal arrangements, even though agreed by the parties concerned, are really just private agreements that have no legal standing. These would include those made with your suppliers to help you over a hump. Formal arrangements are generally legally binding on all parties concerned and involve signed contracts and/or court orders.

1. Refinancing - or in this context, debt refinancing. This is a diffi-cult one to negotiate and usually only really successful if the

owners have anticipated that a shortfall in cash is imminent and are taking viable steps to deal with it. Renegotiating borrowing facilities early enough can make all the difference. But if the company cannot demonstrate they are only experiencing a short-term problem, any borrowing is unlikely to be granted.

2. Voluntary Dissolutions - The owners/directors make the decision to dissolve the company. There can be no outstanding creditors otherwise the company cannot be dissolved. If self-employed, creditors can chase you personally for the money, and even force you to sell your home.

3. CVA/IVA (Company Voluntary Arrangement / Individual Voluntary Arrangement) - Directors/Owners keep control of the company. A CVA and IVA allow a company or individual to pay back their debt, or more specifically a percentage of their debts to their creditors over a specified period of time. Any creditors included in the arrangement are not allowed to chase the company or individual directly as CVA/IVAs are legally binding agreements enforced by the courts. However, while the agreement is in place the company or individual is open to monitoring and scrutiny to ensure business or financial affairs are conducted satisfactorily. Any breach of the rules could result in the CVA or IVA being judged as having failed and the directors could be forced to wind up the company. And the individual forced into bankruptcy

4. Administration and Receivership - Directors lose control of the company. An Insolvency practitioner is appointed by the courts to run the company with a view to protecting the assets and to ensure it continues to trade until a decision about its fate can be made. This could be to sell, refinance, liquidate, go into a CVA, to name but a few options. For this to be feasible, the company must be of a fair size, with cash flow and profits that can be predicted on a fairly reliable basis.

5. Pre-Pack Administration (Grown in popularity). A pre-pack allows the business and its assets to be sold to another party or

even the original directors, without the debts. This allows the business to continue albeit as a brand new company. If the original directors are the buyers, they will need to come up with the money to purchase the assets themselves. In addition it can be seen as the directors avoiding responsibility to the creditors, but if the business was on the verge of collapse the creditors were unlikely to be paid back anyway.

6. Liquidation – The Directors lose control in this case. **Voluntary Liquidation** - The director(s) make the decision to close the company down. Because of outstanding debts it cannot be dissolved, so an Insolvency practitioner is appointed by the directors(s) to close it formally and to deal with the creditors. **Compulsory Liquidation** - as the name suggests. Typically, the company becomes the subject of a winding up order/petition which triggers a visit by the friendly bailiffs.

   I was asked to set up a book-keeping system for a company. While chatting he mentioned that when he tried to make payments using online banking, the payments kept being returned to his account within a couple of days. Thinking it was a technical error, he called the bank only to be told that HMRC had issued a winding up order against the company and his bank accounts had been frozen. It was ironic that he was still able to log on and see his accounts, but not able to use them. As my kids would say "that's cold!"

7. Sale of the Business - The sale of the business can happen at any time - The creditors of a business are free to insist on a sale if a business is already in a CVA, Liquidation or Receivership agreement if they have reason to believe they are more likely to get their money this way rather than the other methods. This by no means guarantees that this will happen, and even if the process begins, a willing buyer still has to be found that will be prepared to buy at a price that enables the creditors to get paid out. Bearing in mind it is a business in trouble, the likelihood of this is slim.

Such a business would be more likely seen as a bargain with plenty of reason to beat the price down.

Wiser but Wary – Dealing with Starting Again

Do you really understand what went wrong before? What were the true causes of the business ultimately failing or becoming insolvent (Unable to pay its bills and debts as and when they are due)?

There is possibly little need to sell the benefits of planning and to implement financial steps to ensure history does not repeat itself.

Do not get too distracted by external reasons. Yes the economy may be or has been bad; and yes good employees are hard to find etc. While not everything that went before was your fault personally, it certainly was your responsibility.

If you live in the belief that your outcomes are due to "they" "things" "situations", you rob yourself of the power of being in control of your future. Acknowledge responsibility, lick your wounds and deal with what you could and can do differently. Limber up those entrepreneurial muscles ready to get going again. This time you have added wisdom to the equation.

Shore up your financial resources. Know what money you need to start again, trade and grow; and plan for how you are going to obtain the necessary funds. In the same way as a start-up would have to. If you are reviving an existing business, it is still prudent to go back to the drawing board and re-evaluate. This is a new beginning.

How good are your personal support systems? Is your husband, wife, boyfriend, girlfriend behind you or have the previous business problems made them more cautious, even resistant to your ambitions? How will this affect you? Are you prepared for the consequences of pursuing something that may cause conflict in your personal life? The support of your nearest and dearest can make a huge difference, they do not necessarily have to be involved, merely understand what you need to do and to back you up.

For the free and single amongst you, having friends and relatives to sound out to is also invaluable.

Have a network of business people you can tap into for motivation and sound advice.

Mix with as many successful business people as you can. There is a different vibe around most successful business people. I am not saying they are all grounded happy people, but can remind you just what is possible in terms of achievement. Who better than those that have been there and done that?

Be honest about your weaknesses in skills, experience and temperament and work out how you are going to combat them.

Be open to advice – from the right people

Mindset change – if you need a coach to help with this then get one.

Arrange training for the people around you to free you up to concentrate on profit and growth tasks.

Outsource and delegate as much as is feasible to build a team of experts around you.

Take a break now and then to recharge your batteries. If you have nailed outsourcing and delegation this should be much easier to do.

As well as going away with friends and family I sometimes disappear for the odd night alone in a nice hotel. Either to get a task done uninterrupted which I call my G1 summit (G1 – get it?), or just to vegetate with my eBook and lots of reading material. Though I am not an avid watcher of television, having the remote to myself is quite a novelty. And of course on tap liquid nourishment. I used to do this even when finances were at their crappiest to remind me what life would be like when I became really established.

Look at your successes and see what can be recreated or built upon. You now have knowledge that you did not have before, even if it is just what not to do. You now also have more experience and more realistic expectations of how business works. This does not mean you lessen your ambitions, it just means you have a better understanding of the steps required to get there.

Do what you need to do to come to terms with the inevitable feelings of failure. If you are struggling with such feelings, be aware that if left unchecked, disappointment can easily manifest itself into depression. Forget about feeling stupid and talk, talk, talk. Enlisting a good coach, as mentioned above; whether purely business, personal or both; are wonderful outlets for working your way through the inevitable hard moments. Do not however, underestimate the value of family and friends. Even if they are not able to solve specific business problems, being able to share in an environment that you feel safe in can be a real help.

Going wrong is part of your exciting journey and not the end of the road.

Stories of how massively successful people originally experienced failure are regularly quoted.

Did you know that Walt Disney was fired from a job working for a newspaper because he apparently had no imagination?

Michael Jordon was dropped from the basketball team while in high school.

Who cannot be aware of the story of Donald Trump experiencing extraordinary business failure and ending up millions in debt before making a remarkable comeback?

The Apprentice that has us glued to our televisions each season, started as his show in the US. From falling star to TV star.

Last Words

Don't give up, and don't be a lone ship in the night.

Whatever you are going through, be it frustration at not being further forward after years of grafting or facing financial meltdown. There are many people that have been through what you are experiencing and come out the other side smiling.

There is no reason why you will not be one of them.

CHAPTER 15

Thank You

I am going to share a little confession.

I always wanted to have something that I could offer to people that was a relatively small cost to them. However because of my need to avoid looking silly; and wanting to include everything but the kitchen sink. The book was delayed longer than necessary.

Now that it is out and I am exposed; it would mean so much to me, if you could take the time and review the book on Amazon.

It would be nice to know if I helped you or not.

To get more free tips, tools and tutorials go to:

www.financialgymforbusiness.com

And I love making new friends so feel free to connect with me on

Facebook: **www.facebook.com/FinancialGymForBusiness**

Twitter: **www.twitter.com/PS_FinancialGym**

Linked In: **uk.linkedin.com/pub/georgette-rowland-osborne-aicb-comp-pm-dip/20/987/774/**

Google+: **plus.google.com/u/0/100193963818853402438/posts**

Best of luck to you
Georgette Rowland Osborne

ACKNOWLEDGMENTS

Where to begin? I want to say thank you to my amazing extended family who are there for each other no matter what. My mother who will still do your ironing and cook your favourite meal to please you; even with her walking stick. A sister you know you can rely on to take care of business when you would rather not, and is just as much a mum to my children as I am. My youngest niece who thinks she was born into a family of nutcases but still joins in. And too many cousins to name but you know you all rock.

My friends that have been there from my childhood and are still in my life today. If walls could talk!

The Mentors that have changed my life with an act of kindness, a gem of information, a kick up the butt and the opportunity to learn from them. Thank you

My amazingly patient editor Annette Young; who helped me take a hidden manuscript and have the courage to put it out into the world

And the lady that will lives by the phrase "No Problem" the utterly awesome Valerie Eaton, an assistant and a half. You are so appreciated.

AMAZING PEOPLE YOU SHOULD KNOW

Who can help you shift your business in a big way

Unless you have been living on another planet, it is unlikely you haven't heard of the likes Steve Jobs, Richard Branson, Oprah Winfrey, Donald Trump etc.

What is great about them is how much they inspire us. But they are at a point of success that is too far removed from most people who are starting out in business or are reinventing their current one. Their day to day is very different from ours.

The purpose of this book is to highlight what is accessible to you *now,* and that includes the experts I mention. There are others throughout the book; but below are a few that have kept me up at night through sheer excitement about what you can get done today.

I really mean today, not when you have enough money, staff, products and any other obstacles that are keeping you stuck where you are.

I mention them not because of their own successes; but because of the work they do to make others successful.

Suzy Greaves

This lady and her work has had quite an impact on me

She is a respected author, journalist, columnist and health editor for some of the most well popular glossy magazines that we know and love. She has navigated her way successfully through many of the challenges of life, relationships and business, and founded The Big Leap Coaching Company which is when I became a fan. She helped me to understand that even coaches need coaches.

When I had one of my dips in life, it was a resource she created that helped me to get on track. More than once I might add. Details of it can be found in the chapter Controlling the Control Freak.

She was very positive and encouraging about my writing this book and sent me a message that gave me a great boost when I needed it. In fact she has a writing course of her own to help authors make their dream a reality. You can visit her site or contact her at

Find her at: **www.suzygreaves.com**

Warren Cass

Warren Cass is a serial entrepreneur, who is so connected it is ridiculous. His database of business owners is so large he has trouble with what most entrepreneurs dream of having; too many offers for joint ventures.

I originally came across Warren because he was always being mentioned by other entrepreneurs in the UK as someone who had given great advice or really helped them in some way to build their business. I have at least 3 books in which he is credited as being a great influence.

Yet he is hands down one of the nicest, most genuine human beings I know and it shows that nice guys do finish first.

He is so fired up about helping small businesses thrive that he built the Business Scene membership organisation as a resource to not just inform; but support its members by finding out what they need, rather than what he wants to sell. They run events all around the UK and the suite of benefits & services far outweighs the membership fee.

Find out more at: **www.business-scene.com/home**

Michael O'Neal

"Job Security for the Unemployable™" If ever there was a perfect mantra for you brave souls taking up the entrepreneurial challenge, that is it. Michael in a very short time has gone from worrying about what to do next with his life to a highly respected mentor. His story about how he went from sleeping on his brother's couch to being approached by big name brands wanting to be his sponsors in a short period of time is so immensely inspiring.

He lives to teach the guy or gal that desperately wants to say goodbye to the 9-5 world; the strategies he used to get there, so they can do it too.

What I love about him is his ability to communicate as a friend and kick you up the butt in one sentence. And with humour. You don't get any more real than Michael.

He has created a very engaged and supportive community of "solopreneurs" as well as a successful podcast and coaching programmes for people going from employment to self-employment.

Find him at: **www.solopreneurhour.com**

Join the community at: **www.solopreneurhour.com/group**

Daniel Priestley the Entrevo Team

Daniel is the author of 2 bestselling books, Key Person of Influence and The Entrepreneur Revolution. With his partner Marcus Ubl and his unstoppable wife Darshana Uble; their Accelerator Programme (Key Person of Influence) has been directly responsible for hundreds of entrepreneurs around the world launching and leveraging their businesses to create game changing entities.

I have never told Daniel this, but the day I sat in a little meeting room with him while he told me to "go own that space" was the beginning of a new life for me. (No doubt he gets told that a lot).

He and Marcus make it clear that what lies ahead is a long hard road; but if you do certain things consistently you will rise up.

Find him at: **www.danielpriestley.com**

Find out about KPI at: **www.keypersonofinfluence.com**

and **www.entrevo.com**

Jeremy Frandsen & Jason Van Orden

They are to online marketing what Charlie Chaplin was to movies. Pioneers.

Not because they invented it of course. In an industry rife with opportunists, and get rich quick schemes; these men created a successful online business that stands out. Why? Because they tell the truth about how they made it. By sheer (and continued) hard work.

They are very real and transparent about their journey from working for someone else to taking control of their own futures.

The ups, the downs, the mistakes, the solutions; and practical ways to move forward when you hit bumps in the road. They have one of longest running and most popular business podcasts on iTunes. They have built a very informative website. Plus a thriving community of entrepreneurs to whom they provide valuable training, resources, guides and support.

One act of personal kindness to me highlights why they are so respected.

Jeremy reached out to me on Twitter a while ago. I was so thrilled I responded like a groupie. (Yeah I know!) I mentioned that I was a fan of his, and also of another entrepreneur, Dan Andrews (see below). Jeremy and I tweeted for a while; and he included, Dan and (the Yoda of online business) Pat Flynn in the conversation to introduce them to me. (Google them).

They used to play Frisbee together. And Pat Flynn attributes much of his start on the road to his phenomenal success to having Jeremy as his coach; and getting the chance to work for him for a year.

Jeremy and Jason never forget how hard it is to transition from employee to being your own boss. To take advantage of their wealth of experience:

Find them at: **www.internetbusinessmastery.com**

Michelle Holmes

Not only is she my beautiful friend but she has transformed the online marketing presence of many celebrities and some of the most successful internet businesses on the planet. She knows how to stand out in a crowded marketplace.

She is uber passionate about helping small businesses; without the budgets of large corporations and celebrities nail their passion. "Find their voice" as she calls it. Particularly with video.

She has the ability to turn a simple idea into money, it is beautiful to watch.

So much so that she has created a business that she can truly run from anywhere in the world with a laptop (and Facebook).

Michelle is singularly one of the most important people in my business world and I have her to thank for clearing the last remnants of employee mentality from my brain.

Find her at: **www.michelle-holmes.com**

Dan Andrews & Ian Schoen

Dan and Ian are two of the most clued up people about business full stop. They have created successful businesses online and offline and manage to do it all while being location independent.

Dan and Ian teach business strategies that can be implemented by individuals and corporations alike and speak in a language that makes you go "hell yeah!" Well I do anyway. They are brilliant at drilling down into the heart of subjects that include business structures, financing, marketing and building relationships. But their success at showing how you can live your dream wherever you live, is priceless.

I became aware of Dan first, after hearing him interviewed. He stood out because he was, and continues to be, a bullshit free zone. If he thinks a business idea or trend is crap, then he will say so. He jokingly admitted to me on Twitter that "he sucked at playing Frisbee" (see Jeremy Frandsen and Jason Van Orden above) but made up for it with an uncanny understanding of the dynamics of making money. If I could carry him and Ian around in my bag during the day to tap for advice, I most certainly would.

Find them at: **www.tropicalmba.com**

Lisa & Anthony Charles

I first met Lisa and Anthony at an event they co-hosted hosted by legendary entrepreneur Ron Holland. (The man bought www.wealth.co.uk as a domain name before we had even heard of Google and is responsible for creating many other millionaires).

With Ron's mentoring Lisa and Anthony turned a back bedroom dream into a real magazine called Choices. Choices Magazine is aimed at what Anthony calls "employee-preneurs". People who are trying find resources to help them make the transition from employee to entrepreneur.

Each issue is a series of articles by various entrepreneurs and thought leaders. Each article must have relevant, actionable tips that the reader can use straight away.

Lisa and Anthony's vision for employee-preneurs is to make the transition from employee and entrepreneur easy and to make the dream of having a thriving business of your own a reality.

To find out more visit: **www.choicesmagazine.co.uk**

www.ingramcontent.com/pod-product-compliance
Lightning Source LLC
Chambersburg PA
CBHW060930050726

47592CB00003B/892